Enhancing University Teaching

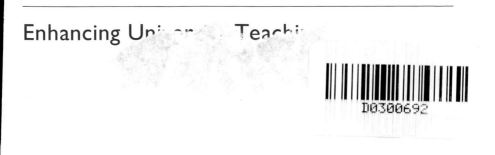

In response to demands upon universities to improve the quality of teaching, several governments have attempted to find acceptable measures of what constitutes good university teaching, but have had difficulty doing so. Educational theorists have derived many models of good teaching which diverge widely.

Enhancing University Teaching aims to fill this vacuum by deriving a model of good university teaching from 62 academics, chosen by their universities as their best teachers. These award-winning teachers encompass all major discipline areas and interviews with them have resulted in ten common principles of good university teaching. These include:

- Ensure that students have a thorough understanding of fundamental concepts, if necessary at the expense of covering excessive content.
- Meaningful learning is most likely to occur when students are actively engaged with a variety of learning tasks.
- Establishing empathetic relationships with students is a pre-requisite to successful interaction with them.
- Thorough planning is needed for each lesson, but plans need to be adapted flexibly in the light of feedback obtained in class.
- Assessment must be consistent with the desired learning outcomes and eventual student needs if these are to be achieved.

Packed with practical and detailed advice on how to be a good university teacher and help students achieve desired learning outcomes, this book is essential reading for any academic wanting to enhance the quality of their own teaching.

David Kember is currently Professor of Learning Enhancement at The Chinese University of Hong Kong. **Carmel McNaught** is Director of the Centre for Learning Enhancement And Research and Professor of Learning Enhancement at The Chinese University of Hong Kong.

Enhancing University Teaching

Lessons from research into
award-winning teachers

David Kember with
Carmel McNaught

Routledge
Taylor & Francis Group

LONDON AND NEW YORK

First published 2007
by Routledge
2 Park Square, Milton Park, Abingdon, Oxon OX14 4RN

Simultaneously published in the USA and Canada
by Routledge
270 Madison Ave, New York, NY 10016

Routledge is an imprint of the Taylor & Francis Group, an informa business

Typeset in Times and Gill by BC Typesetting Ltd, Bristol
Printed and bound in Great Britain by
TJ International Ltd, Padstow, Cornwall

British Library Cataloguing in Publication Data
A catalogue record for this book is available from the British Library

Library of Congress Cataloging in Publication Data
A catalog record has been requested for this book

ISBN10: 0–415–41716–3 (hbk)
ISBN10: 0–415–42025–3 (pbk)

ISBN13: 978–0–415–41716–7 (hbk)
ISBN13: 978–0–415–42025–9 (pbk)

Contents

Acknowledgements   vii
Principles of good teaching   viii
Downloading resource materials   x

1 Introduction   1

2 Method   5

PART I
What is good teaching?   9

3 Generalisability of perceptions of quality in teaching   11

4 Aims   18

5 What to teach   33

6 How to teach   44

7 Motivating students   51

PART II
Principles into practice   59

8 Planning courses and lessons   61

9 Teaching large classes   72

10 Managing discussion and group-work   83

11 Ways of encouraging active learning   97

12 Assessment   114

PART III
Developing as a teacher

Developing as a teacher   133

13 Influences on good teachers   135
14 Obtaining feedback   142
15 Conclusion   155

   References   160
   Index   164

Acknowledgements

To properly acknowledge everyone who has contributed to this book it is necessary to tell something of the somewhat unusual story of how it came to be written. The project started with Carmel McNaught obtaining a generous grant from the directly assigned portion of the University Grant Committee of Hong Kong's Teaching Development Grants from The Chinese University of Hong Kong (CUHK). The funding was used to employ Rosa Ma to conduct interviews with 18 teachers who had been awarded the Vice-Chancellor's Award for Exemplary Teaching. The 18 teachers were David Ahlstrom, Andrew Chan, Francis Chan, Chan Hung Kan, Gregory Cheng, Gordon Cheung, Chu Ming Chung, Fan Jianqing, Patrick Lau, John Chi Kin Lee, Kenneth Leung, Leung Sing Fai, Soung Liew, Lo Wai Luen, John Lui, Gordon Mathews, Allan Walker and Zhang Shuzhong.

The initiative was inspired by a project by Roy Ballantyne, John Bain and Jan Packer who had produced a set of 44 stories of outstanding teachers in Australia. The initial aim of the CUHK project had been to produce a similar set of stories. They turned out, though, to be rather too similar. I then came on the scene and started to analyse the interviews for common themes. This worked well; so we ended up with a booklet of principles of good teaching by award-winning CUHK teachers, which has proved invaluable for professional development purposes in the University. The activities included in the book were developed by Carmel and myself for the many courses we have offered for new teachers and teaching assistants.

The CUHK work, though, would have limited credibility with an international audience; so we were pleased when Roy Ballantyne, John Bain and Jan Packer encouraged us to make use of their stories. As the Australian stories were more diverse, and many concentrated in detail on particular topics, it was possible to produce a much more comprehensive treatise on good teaching practices. The numerous quotations included are acknowledged as being derived from Roy, John and Jan's book by citing B B & P and the original page number. The teacher is also acknowledged by name and institution.

I would like to thank John Biggs for giving permission to reproduce the revised version of the Study Process Questionnaire and the diagrams representing the SOLO categories.

David Kember

Principles of good teaching

In this book a set of ten principles of good teaching are derived, explained and illustrated. The principles (numbered by chapter) are listed below to provide a preview and to help readers deal with the frequent cross-referencing.

4.1 Teaching and curriculum design needs to be consistent with meeting students' future needs. This implies the development of a range of generic capabilities including:

- self-managed learning ability,
- critical thinking,
- analytical skills,
- team-work,
- leadership, and
- communication skills.

5.1 Ensure that students have a thorough understanding of fundamental concepts, if necessary at the expense of covering excessive content.

5.2 Establish the relevance of what is taught by:

- using real-life examples,
- drawing cases from current issues,
- giving local examples, and
- relating theory to practice.

5.3 Challenging beliefs is important to:

- establish appropriate ways of learning and beliefs about knowledge, and
- deal with misconceptions of fundamental concepts.

6.1 Meaningful learning is most likely to occur when students are actively engaged with a variety of learning tasks. Discussion is an important learning activity.

6.2 Establishing empathetic relationships with students is a pre-requisite to successful interaction with them. To do this you need to know them as individuals.

7.1 Good teachers accept that it is their responsibility to motivate students to achieve the high expectations they have of them. Motivation comes through:

- encouraging students,
- the enthusiasm of the teacher,
- interesting and enjoyable classes,
- relevant material, and
- a variety of active learning approaches.

8.1 Planning programmes and courses involves consideration of students' future needs. The plans ensure that aims, fundamental concepts, learning activities and assessment are consistent with achieving outcomes related to future student needs. Feedback needs to be gathered to inform each of these elements in the curriculum design process.

8.2 Thorough planning is needed for each lesson, but plans need to be adapted flexibly in the light of feedback obtained in class.

12.1 Assessment must be consistent with the desired learning outcomes and eventual student needs if these are to be achieved. Assessment should, therefore, be authentic tasks for the discipline or profession.

DOWNLOADING RESOURCE MATERIAL

Readers are invited to download and use the resources listed below for evaluating their teaching, for use in workshops and taught courses and for genuine research purposes. The conditions are that they acknowledge the source as this book, accept the copyright ownership as listed below, and, for the case of the Revised Study Process Questionnaire, give the following reference as that for the original publication of the questionnaire.

Biggs, J., Kember, D. and Leung, D. Y. P. (2001). The revised two factor Study Process Questionnaire: R-SPQ-2F. *British Journal of Educational Psychology*, 71, 133–149.

Revised Study Process Questionnaire   Ch. 4
© 2001 John Biggs and David Kember

Scoring key for the R-SPQ   Ch. 4
© 2006 David Kember and Carmel McNaught

Course planning grid   Ch. 8
© 2006 Carmel McNaught and David Kember

Class planning grid   Ch. 8
© 2006 David Kember and Carmel McNaught

Reflection checklist for lectures   Ch. 9
© 2006 Carmel McNaught and David Kember

Do you spend too much time lecturing?   Ch. 9
© 2006 David Kember and Carmel McNaught

Reflection checklist for seminars and tutorials   Ch. 10
© 2006 Carmel McNaught and David Kember

Course planning grid, including assessment   Ch. 12
© 2006 David Kember and Carmel McNaught

Course Questionnaire based on the principles of good teaching   Ch. 14
© 2006 David Kember and Doris Y.P. Leung

Course Questionnaire based on the principles of good teaching   Ch. 14
(Full Version)
© 2006 David Kember and Doris Y.P. Leung

Chapter 1

Introduction

Good teaching

Governments, employers and students all over the world have been making demands upon universities to improve the quality of teaching. As a result academics have been required or encouraged to engage in a range of activities to make them better teachers. Examples are formal courses, staff development workshops, quality assurance reviews and grants for projects to introduce innovative forms of teaching.

An issue which has constantly dogged the drive for quality in teaching is the question of what is good teaching? When accountability became an important issue several governments formed bodies to devise a concise way to monitor, or preferably measure, the quality of teaching in a department or university. The hope was that there would be something similar to the way in which research quality is determined by the number of publications and the value of grants awarded. However, teaching quality proved to be a very complex construct, and so the various committees did not produce the neat definitions and performance indicators the governments were hoping for.

Models of good teaching have been derived from educational theories. The problem with these is that there are many diverse educational theories. The models of good teaching derived from contrasting theories can be quite different in nature. Good practice according to traditional behavioural theory can be poor practice from a social constructivist stance. To compound the problem many academics have little respect for any educational theory.

This book aims to fill this vacuum by deriving a model of good university teaching from the academics which universities have chosen as their best teachers, those who were selected for the exemplary teaching awards which most universities now give. These awards are almost always based on substantial input from academic colleagues and extensive student feedback. The practices of these award-winning teachers can, therefore, legitimately be claimed to be good practice in teaching in the eyes of their university community.

The award-winning teachers featured in this book included 44 from universities in Australia (Ballantyne, Bain and Packer, 1997). These came from 25 universities, with the selection process open to the entire Australian university system. The remaining 18 award-winning teachers were from The Chinese University of Hong Kong (CUHK). The sample is, therefore, extensive by the standards of qualitative research and diverse in being drawn from the East and a multicultural country in the West.

Each of the 62 award-winning teachers was interviewed, at some length, about their beliefs and practices as a teacher. The interviewees were talking about a topic on which they were interested and often passionate; as a result, the transcripts were rich in detailed descriptions of good practice and insights into why they had been chosen as exemplary teachers.

From the interview transcripts a story was produced for each of the 62 award-winning teachers. Teachers' narratives or stories have been reasonably widely used in research into school teachers, but less commonly applied to higher education. They constitute a case which retains the disciplinary and contextual richness. They can reveal both the practices of teachers and the beliefs, values and aims which underpin them. Elbaz (1991, p. 3) argued that:

> Story is the very stuff of teaching, the landscape within which we live as teachers and researchers, and within which the work of teachers can be seen as making sense. This is not merely a claim about the aesthetic or emotional sense of fit of the notion of a story with our intuitive understanding of teaching, but an epistemological claim that teachers' knowledge can best be understood in this way.

These stories were then analysed by the conventional qualitative data analysis techniques of grounded theory and the constant comparative method. The aim was to look for common constructs relating to teaching quality. Coding and sorting of the data led towards an analytical framework outlining the constituents of good practice in teaching.

Analysis of teachers' stories provides the reader with a framework of common themes or principles, while retaining the richness of the underlying stories. Analysis without the stories can lead to decontextualisation. The stories without the analysis leave it to the reader to perform the demanding task of searching for insights into common issues and practices.

The process of analysis was a way of deriving theory from the stories. The theory of this book is, therefore, derived from the practice of award-winning university teachers. The sampling was wide and diverse and the analysis rigorous; so the theory has to be accepted as credible, valid and reliable. It is also practical and usable theory as it comes from university teachers themselves. The stories are insights into what award-winning teachers see as good teaching and the type of teaching they have found to work best and be most effective in achieving the student learning outcomes they feel are appropriate. As the teachers come from diverse backgrounds and disciplines, the outcomes should be credible to academics.

This book differs from others about teaching in higher education which derive their theory and advice on practice from the educational research literature. These books are usually replete with references. By contrast this book has fewer references but numerous quotations from the award-winning teachers.

The outcome of the analysis was a set of principles of good teaching practice. Given the diversity of the sample there was a remarkably high degree of consistency to the principles. There was no evidence of any cultural disparity between East and West, indicating perhaps that academics in reputable universities constitute an international culture. The set of principles of good university teaching can, therefore, be seen as having international applicability.

Principles

The principles of good teaching are shown in a text box in this format at the point at which they are derived. They are also collected together as a set in the Conclusion.

The Australian sample came from each of the types of university in the Australian system and there were representatives from just about every major type of discipline. CUHK is a comprehensive university and the award-winners were selected from every faculty. Readers should, then, be able to relate very closely to the issues raised by award-winning teachers in fields closely related to their own.

In the book the principles are explained, justified and illuminated through extensive quotations from the stories. The often graphic comments should persuade most academics that the principles are worthy of being followed. The detailed accounts of practice should enable others to put these principles into practice by following in the footsteps of the award-winning teachers.

Pedagogical features

The material contained in the book has already been used in formal courses and staff-development workshops within our own University. Principles, quotations and examples have been taken directly from the stories for the courses and workshops. This material has provided a very successful framework for these sessions. Teachers really sit up and take note when a course is based on the stories of the best teachers in their country or university.

In addition to deriving principles and examples from the stories, the formal courses have tried to model good practice by adopting a teaching approach consistent with the derived principles of good teaching. Among other things, this has meant adopting an active learning approach, in which the teachers engage in activities to reflect on their own practice as teachers.

Most of these activities, and some additional ones, have been included in the book, with modification to suit the different mode. Some of these activities are best suited to small groups of teachers taking a course in teaching in higher education. This book is therefore ideal as a set text for such courses. Other activities are designed for reflection on practice by the individual teacher. Most could be undertaken by individuals or groups.

Activities

Activities are indicated by text boxes in this format.

Further readings are suggested to provide greater information about teaching methods and to provide background material from the literature when this might be useful. These further readings are normally annotated to indicate their purpose to the reader. The following format is used for further readings.

Annotation

Reference

To facilitate the use of this book as a set text for courses and workshops for teachers, an accompanying website at

http://www.routledge.com/textbooks/9780415420259

has copies of resource material for the activities, which can be downloaded for educational purposes. Resources which are included on the website are indicated in the following format:

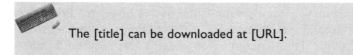

The [title] can be downloaded at [URL].

Chapter 2

Method

This chapter is kept quite brief and without excessive detail. The main purpose of the book is as a text for courses in teaching in higher education
and for individual academics who want to improve their teaching. The aim
of this chapter is to provide just sufficient information about the method
of the study to convince the reader that the conclusions drawn are valid
and reliable.

The method is presented in chronological order. The study can perhaps
best be described as one which evolved as opportunities were presented,
experience was gained and frameworks unfolded. It was certainly not a
study which started with a detailed research design which was followed to
the letter.

Stories

The first initiative of relevance was a project by Ballantyne, Bain and Packer
(1997) which constructed stories from interviews with 44 Australian academics nominated by their universities as being exemplary or noteworthy
teachers. The selected academics came from a wide range of disciplines
and universities.

Each academic participated in a quite open interview which resembled a
guided conversation. The interviewees were asked to describe their teaching practices and the beliefs which underpinned them. The stories were
conducted from the interviews with the aim of retaining as much of the interviewees' own words as was consistent with producing coherent prose.
The outcome was a published volume consisting of the set of 44 stories
(Ballantyne et al., 1997).

This served as an inspiration for Carmel McNaught to start a project at
The Chinese University of Hong Kong (CUHK) to conduct interviews with
18 recipients of the Vice-Chancellor's award for exemplary teaching, awarded
in the first three years of its operation, 1999–2001. These interviews were
conducted by Rosa Ma. Again, the interviews followed a conversational

semi-structured format. Twelve of these interviews were conducted in Cantonese.

Translation was required for the majority of the transcripts. Stories were produced in a form which again preserved the sense of the interviews as far as possible. The intention had been to produce a similar volume consisting of a set of stories. At this point, though, doubts arose as to whether this was the most useful form of publication. By emanating from the same university, the CUHK stories lacked the diversity of the Australian ones.

There were also considerations of whether the intended audience of other academics would make use of the stories. To find insights valuable for their own teaching, each reader would have to do their own search and analysis. It seemed likely that most readers would find it more helpful if the stories were analysed for consistent themes and common practices among the award-winning teachers.

Analysis of the CUHK stories

An analysis was, therefore, conducted of the CUHK stories. The widely used qualitative data analysis technique of grounded theory (Glaser and Straus, 1967; Lincoln and Guber, 1985) was used. Grounded theory assumes that the research starts without hypotheses or preconceived theories, instead the researcher searches the data for common constructs or theories. In this way theory is derived from the data and can be said to be grounded in it. Use was also made of the constant comparative method (Strauss and Corbin, 1990) which involves checking thematic phrases against the complete transcript to ensure that an extract is consistent with the sense of the whole. This provides a guard against misinterpretation or taking comments out of context.

In practice this meant reading and rereading the thick pile of transcripts searching for commonality and points of significance. As these started to become apparent, coding notes were pencilled into the margin. The codings were then successively expanded and refined.

Use was then made of NVivo, a computer program for aiding the processes of analysing qualitative data (NVivo, 2000; Richards and Richards, 1991). The set of pencil codings on paper were converted to NVivo codes on the files of the transcripts. The coding scheme employed a hierarchical tree structure to show the relationship between the coded themes. The program was then used to sort the data according to the codes, producing a revised dataset containing the highlighted material, ordered so that parts given the same code appear together.

This revised dataset was then re-examined to revise the hierarchical structure and to make the analysis more fine-grained by the addition of subcategories or codes where appropriate. The NVivo files were then modified to match the revised coding. A file was then produced which would serve as a basis for the final part of the analysis of the CUHK data, which was the writing process. In the writing, principles of good teaching were derived from themes which were found to be consistent across the stories. These were explained and illustrated by typical quotations.

Verification procedures were used to check the conclusions. The stories had been verified by the interviewees. It was possible to check the NVivo file to see what proportion of the CUHK interviewees had made comments consistent with a principle or theme. This provided a semi-quantitative verification of key points, and at points in the following text these figures are given. It should be noted that these are an underestimate of the level of agreement with a construct, as interviews are not exhaustive and the interviewee might agree with a point, but had not raised it. As chapters were completed they were sent to each of the interviewees to check that their views were consistent with the final analysis. As all responses were dealt with, it can be said with confidence that the beliefs and practices of the CUHK award-winning teachers had been accurately captured by the analysis and that there was a high degree of consistency about them.

Becoming multicultural

This analysis of the stories of the CUHK award-winning teachers has been published as Kember, Ma, McNaught and 18 excellent teachers (2006). While this should provide a valuable resource for teachers at CUHK, it is unlikely to reach a significant readership outside the University. Evidence is given in the book that university teachers in reputable universities subscribe to an international culture. This, though, is unlikely to offset suspicions, particularly from those in the West, as to whether award-winning teachers at one university in Hong Kong constitute a viable model for their own practice as teachers.

Permission was, therefore, sought from the authors of the volume of Australian teachers' stories (Ballantyne et al., 1997) to combine the two sets of stories with the aim of analysing them to see if a similar set of common constructs could be unveiled. If that were the case, it would be possible to produce a book which could legitimately claim that its conclusions were not context-dependent, as they had been derived from a large and diverse multicultural sample of award-winning teachers.

A similar process of grounded analysis was then performed on half of the Australian stories. Odd-numbered chapters were chosen to provide a representative half, as the stories were ordered in the book by discipline. The analysis was conducted from first principles, but it would be surprising if there was not some carry over of insights from the analysis of the CUHK data.

It transpired that the analytical coding hierarchy for the Australian stories was compatible with the CUHK one, but contained additional categories because some of the Australian stories were wider in scope. This argument can be verified by the typical quotations selected which are a mix from both Australia and CUHK. It will be seen that the important principles can be substantiated by typical quotations from both sets of interviews. Having verified that a consistent analytical framework could be applied to both datasets, the remaining even-numbered chapters were then examined for useful insights consistent with the established principles.

Part I

What is good teaching?

Generalisability of perceptions of quality in teaching

Quality in teaching

This book is a textbook which offers advice to university teachers on how to improve the quality of their teaching. The advice has been derived from interviews with 62 award-winning teachers. The thesis on which the book is based is that the students and colleagues of these teachers have determined their teaching to be of such a high standard that they have been recognised as deserving an award for exemplary teaching from their universities. These teachers, then, are suitable to be models for other university teachers. Readers who follow the advice and practice of these excellent teachers should be able to improve the quality of their own teaching.

An important condition for this premise to be viable is that there is a reasonable degree of consistency about the practice of the award-winning teachers. The analysis of the interview transcripts commenced with an open examination, with no pre-set hypotheses of what principles of good teaching might be found. There was sufficient commonality in the interviews that common themes could be extracted. Chapter 2 has outlined the methodological procedures adopted to ensure that these common themes were generalisable across the substantial and diverse sample.

It is also important that it is credible that this degree of consistency is applicable to university teachers outside the sample. In other words, readers need to believe that the advice is generalisable and not restricted in applicability to particular cultures or relevant only to the discipline of the original teacher. This chapter examines the literature on variability or consistency of indicators of quality in university teaching. In particular, there is an examination of possible variations across disciplines or between cultures, which are perhaps the two most likely sources of inconsistency.

Award schemes for exemplary teachers

As the principal analysis of the book utilises interviews with award-winning teachers, it seems reasonable to start with an examination of research into the recipients of awards for exemplary university teaching. Schemes of this type have become very common. Ramsden and colleagues (1995) reported that 62 per cent of Australian universities surveyed in their report on 'Recognising and rewarding good teaching in Australian higher education' had a scheme for awarding excellent teachers.

While schemes for rewarding exemplary teachers have become commonplace, it is surprising how few research studies there are of award-winning university teachers. Dunkin and Precians (1992) interviewed 12 award-winning teachers and compared their comments with those of novice teachers. The results are discussed further in Dunkin (2002). The study identified four main dimensions as being common to effective teaching: structuring learning, motivating learning, encouraging activity and independence, and establishing interpersonal relationships. These dimensions were an appropriate category scheme for both experts and novices. The distinction between experts and novices was that the former showed a greater frequency in mentioning the dimensions.

Ballantyne et al. (1997) conducted the interviews with 44 exemplary teachers used as part of the material for this book. The interviews were with teachers from a diverse range of disciplines in Australian universities. The book contained individual stories from each of the 44 teachers. The authors also looked for some common themes across the stories (Ballantyne et al., 1997, pp. xix–xxxiv; 1999). The analysis was reported as dominant themes, which were not present in each story, but there was no evidence of distinctions by discipline, type of university or other variables.

Bain (2004) conducted a 15-year study of the thinking and practices of highly successful university educators in the US. In this detailed study he used interviews, observations, curriculum statements and materials. This rich data set results in an essay about the practices of 63 selected excellent teachers. Again the author managed to find a high degree of commonality in the practice of the successful teachers.

While the studies of excellent teachers are few in number, each has been able to find commonality in the practices of good teachers. None have reported distinctions in conceptions of the quality of teaching by discipline or other relevant category. Research into award-winning teachers, therefore, lends credibility to the idea that notions of quality in university teaching can be generalised.

University teachers' beliefs about teaching

While there has been a reasonably limited amount of research into the practices and beliefs of award-winning teachers, there has been more research into the beliefs about teaching of university teachers in general. Kember (1997) reviewed 13 studies of university teachers' conceptions of teaching.

Ten of the 13 studies examined in the review gathered data through interviews with academics at universities in Australia and the UK. Two (Gow and Kember, 1993; Kember and Gow, 1994) collected data from universities in Hong Kong. The sample for the remaining study (Pratt, 1992) was from Canada, China, Hong Kong, Singapore and the USA. The review did not find differences between categories of beliefs about teaching conceptions between the studies in Western universities and those in Asia. None of the individual studies had identified disciplinary differences.

Rather than finding differences by discipline or culture, it was in fact possible to produce a synthesised multiple-level model which subsumed all the reviewed research on beliefs about teaching in the 13 studies (Kember, 1997). The model contained five categories of beliefs subsumed under two broad orientations; one labelled teacher-centred/content-oriented, and the other student-centred/learning-oriented. These orientations and categories were shown to be reasonably consistent with all 13 studies, suggesting international applicability.

Chinese conceptions of teaching?

Subsequent to this 1997 review, a paper by Pratt, Kelly and Wong (1999) claimed to have identified a distinct Chinese conception of effective university teaching. The essence of this conception is captured by the following quotation.

> The primary responsibility of a teacher was to take students systematically through a clear set of tasks, high in structure and directed towards examination. As the first step, students are expected to copy, drill and memorize the basics, or 'foundational' knowledge of their discipline in forms that closely resemble its presentation by the teacher and/or the text. The process of memorization was understood to be both purposeful and appropriate.
>
> (Pratt et al., 1999, p. 248)

This conception is completely at odds with the principles derived from the interviews with the award-winning CUHK teachers and also inconsistent with the Kember (1997) review and the studies reviewed in it. The incompatibility of the claims of Pratt and colleagues (1999) with other research can be explained by considering their sampling and analytical methods, though these are not explained as clearly as they might be. Their data were mostly gathered through a survey with open-ended questions. Responses were received from 397 students and 82 academic staff, with a response rate of just 14 per cent from the latter. The breakdown of academic staff into the Chinese and Western samples is not reported, but Westerners are a small minority in universities in Hong Kong. Whatever the split, the Chinese sample would have been dominated by students and these would have been compared to a handful of Western academics.

The disparity in sampling was then compounded by the analytical procedure adopted which is reported as: 'our findings are presented as differences between extremes' (p. 245). Chinese conceptions of teaching, therefore, effectively come from students, whereas Western conceptions of teaching come from a limited number of professors teaching in universities in Hong Kong. The conceptions of teaching of the Chinese sample, who are predominantly Chinese students, are then attributed to all Chinese teachers and students.

It is not surprising that a sample dominated by students could hold predominant beliefs of the type attributed by Pratt and colleagues (1999). Hong Kong still has an elite higher education system; as a consequence, secondary schools place a high priority on preparing their students to perform well in the all-important examinations. Most school students, therefore, have a great deal of exposure to didactic teaching which aims to ensure that they will be able to answer questions which are likely to appear in the examinations. The following quotation for the interview with one of the CUHK award-winning teachers illustrates this point well.

> At university level, being able to understand well and yet be good at exams are two separate things. There are students who are excellent in exams in secondary level but only average in faculty exams. Their clinical performance and communication can be rather poor. This is due to the different requirements at university level. At secondary level, they are required to memorise a lot and to regurgitate during exams. At university level, it is not simply how much you memorise but, rather, how much you understand and how effectively you can convey your understanding. In the Faculty of Medicine, students have to face such tremendous amount of stuff to learn that they may not be able to prioritise their learning according to the degree of importance. Their problem with examinations is even greater. Our exams stress the ability to communicate. When they have a deficit in these skills and techniques in communicating, these are very hard for them to acquire.
>
> In our first meeting with students, I will tell them: You should throw away your accustomed ways of learning at secondary schools; otherwise, you will be banging your head against a great wall, and wondering why I was always top of the class in secondary schools and, now, I'm struggling to get by!
>
> (Francis Chan – CUHK – Medicine and Therapeutics)

There is an interpretation of the data from the study of Pratt and colleagues (1999) which is consistent with the Kember's (1997) review. This position is that both of the main teaching–belief orientations exist in

China, as they do in universities elsewhere. The teacher-centred/content-oriented belief predominated in the study of Pratt and colleagues (1999) because their Hong Kong sample was mostly students. The teachers interviewed in the studies reviewed by Kember (1997) showed both orientations because they were reasonably representative samples. Although conceptions of teaching were not specifically examined in the interviews used to provide the data for this book, where beliefs can be inferred they are of the student-centred/learning-oriented orientation, because the samples were award-winning teachers.

Cultural boundaries of teaching practice

The evidence presented so far in this chapter has suggested that beliefs and practices of university teachers, with respect to the quality of teaching, are not culturally specific. There is, though, some evidence that those of school teachers are. Stigler and Hiebert (1999) compared school teaching in Germany, Japan and the US by video-taping classrooms in the three countries. The conclusion which is relevant to this work is that they 'were amazed at how much teaching varied across cultures and how little it varied within cultures' (p. 11).

The conclusion of Stigler and Hiebert (1999) is compatible with the findings of the previous sections of this chapter if the cultural boundaries are carefully defined. The first position to establish is that there is little or no cultural influence between school and university teachers in a particular culture. The practices and ideals of school and university teachers are sufficiently different to conclude that they are not part of a common culture.

University professors and school teachers have always been regarded as quite distinct professions. School teachers tend to have a national rather than an international outlook, and so it is not surprising that there are distinct cultures between school teaching in different countries. It is also reasonable to assume that these cultures have limited impact on university teachers in a particular country, who are themselves part of a quite distinct international university culture. Kenneth Leung's observations show that he is convinced that teaching at school is quite different to that at university.

> I always challenge my students that university education should not be the same as secondary education. Students should not only know how to answer questions, but also how to ask questions. You can ask only if you know where the problem is. Can you identify problems from the superficial facts or phenomena? Lots of teachers can't help students in that sense until they are trained. Therefore, I think my subject helps students challenge the cases given to them.
>
> One of the main purposes of my teaching is enhancing those undergraduate students' understanding of university education. It is not

something they can comfortably sit with. They should rigorously challenge their own conventional thinking. The way they think, the way they look at observable phenomenon so as to be able to learn how to learn. That's the crux of learning how to learn, the ability to identify the problem. If you are able to ask questions, you will find the answers.

They are learning not only to get credits but also how to face the data, observable phenomenon and decision-making. That's why the most frequent comment in both undergraduate and graduate students' course evaluation is 'highly inspirational'. It is exciting. I think it is from students who don't have sufficient preparation for this kind of training.

(Kenneth Leung – CUHK – Journalism)

University teachers as an international culture

There would appear to be a logic to ascribing university teachers to an international culture, which applies to those in universities of a reputable international standard. As universities have been founded it has been common practice for them to try to strengthen their reputation by striving to follow as far as possible the configuration of universities held in the highest regard. In this respect Oxbridge and the Ivy League universities have served as a model for practice, even if the ideal has not always been reached.

Procedures for maintaining standards across university systems serve to reinforce the cultural uniformity of striving for a common model. For example, the external examiner system, which has been widely adopted in the British Commonwealth, was introduced with the rationale of achieving uniformity of degree standards across universities. Such a quality assurance system can only operate if there is a degree of homogeneity in the practices of universities.

The influence of overseas university systems is strengthened through academics receiving education overseas. Of the 15 Chinese CUHK excellent teachers, 12 took at least one of their degrees in overseas universities. This time in overseas universities is particularly important in the light of the comments quoted in Chapter 14, which show that former teachers had one of the strongest influences on their development as teachers.

I did my PhD abroad. . . . I remember when I was in Graduate School (UCLA), there was a course that started at 8 in the morning. For a lot of students, it's hard to get up and attend a lecture at 8 a.m. But every time I came out of his lecture, I felt packed with energy and ready for the day. He taught something very abstract. In the last lesson, when he announced that the course was over, all the students gave him a standing ovation.

(John Lui – CUHK – Computer Science and Engineering)

Disciplinary tribes

While the studies of beliefs about teaching showed no disciplinary distinctions, there is a significant literature arguing that academics associate closely with their discipline. The most prominent advocate is probably Becher (1989), who likened disciplines to academic tribes. Interestingly this visualisation provides further evidence of the globalisation of academia. If disciplines are to be regarded as akin to a tribe, it is definitely an international tribe. Members of the tribe work towards the common icon of publications in the more prestigious journals. International networks form through contacts at tribal gatherings, or conferences, and are then reinforced in this era of information technology.

The main focus of the disciplinary tribes is on research. Meetings at conferences are to discuss research and the communications they share through journals and newsgroups are predominantly about research.

If there is a tribal concern about teaching, the concentration is probably on what is taught. Many disciplines have a reasonably common core of basic knowledge which most syllabi would include. There might also be discussion within the tribe about the inclusion of recent advances in the field in more specialised courses.

The sections above have indicated, though, that disciplinary tribes do not differ significantly in terms of their vision of what constitutes quality in teaching. This is perhaps not surprising as the topic is rarely debated within disciplines other than education. Membership of a discipline can be seen as a strong influence on other elements of academia, but not on issues dealt with in this book.

Conclusion

This chapter has reviewed a number of strands of research evidence which suggest that there is no valid evidence of cultural distinctions over the way academics envisage good teaching. Instead a compelling argument can be made for viewing academics in reputable universities as an international community with respect to quality in teaching. There are also no grounds for believing that quality teaching is envisioned in differing ways according to discipline.

The principles of good teaching, derived in this book, can be regarded as applicable to university teaching in general. The advice of the award-winning teachers can be seen as useful and applicable regardless of the reader's discipline or culture.

Chapter 4

Aims

This is the first of the chapters which focuses principally on deriving principles of good teaching. Logically enough, the first such chapter seeks a sense of direction by examining the aims or goals which underpin good teaching. The theme of the book is deriving principles and practice in good teaching from the stories of 62 award-winning teachers. Typical quotations taken directly from the stories will be used to explain and illustrate important concepts. The first of many such quotations is used at this point to justify taking the aims of teaching as a starting point. The quotations from Ballantyne, Bain and Packer (1997) are referred to as B B & P.

> I would define good teaching as teaching that has a stated aim for what the students are going to learn or be able to do at the end that they couldn't do at the beginning, and that successfully achieves that aim. So I define good teaching in terms of aims and achievements rather than in terms of using particular methods.
>
> (Alan Butler – Adelaide – Zoology, B B & P, p. 288)

Student needs

The starting point for determining the aims of programmes and courses is student needs. What knowledge, skills and capabilities do students need on graduation?

> We have students in our minds when designing courses: What will students want to learn? Why are these skills and ideas useful for them in the future? The courses are primarily designed for students. We want to educate them so that they can go out to the real world and work with the tools and techniques they have learnt. From time to time, we also launch very specific, focused areas, and this always gauges the demand of the students.
>
> (Fan Jianqing – CUHK – Statistics)

On a point of terminology, we will use the term *programme* to refer to a degree such as a BSc. The term *course* will then be used for the constituent parts of a programme, normally lasting for a semester or term.

In professional programmes, like teaching, this implies that the students need to graduate competent as a professional in the field. Knowing theories about teaching is not sufficient – the students need to be able to put theory into practice.

> I will select teaching theory that is practical to my students' everyday teaching life. In addition to teaching plain theory, I apply examples of teaching experiences in high schools. I would like to integrate theory with teaching experiences. To facilitate better understanding, I also arrange the class venue like a real classroom setting.
>
> (Patrick Lau – CUHK – Educational Psychology)

Setting aims in terms of the knowledge, skills and capabilities students will need on graduation is probably not the most common starting point in planning university programmes and courses. Course outlines often consist of lists of content, implying that the course planning has been based on considering what content will be covered. The danger of this approach is that the courses all too often become over-stuffed with content, much of which goes out one ear as fast as it goes in the other.

> I often ask my students when they begin training as teachers how much they remember of what they learned at school. The answer is, almost invariably, 'pitifully little'. I wonder how much of the knowledge our students get at university they are actually going to need.
>
> (Wendy Crebbin – Ballarat – Education, B B & P, p. 145)

Learning to learn

The first skill or competence needed by students is an ability to learn on their own. On graduation they need to be lifelong or self-managed learners; so this ability needs to be developed. This aim is reinforced by the stress on active engagement in learning which is introduced as a principle in Chapter 6.

> I've become more open to my students, let them develop their independent thinking through my teaching and guidance. I would tell them, 'These are the authors and their backgrounds. Can you put your feet into their shoes and enter into their lives through their writings, how they lived in their times?'
>
> (Lo Wai Luen – CUHK – Chinese Literature)

Developing the ability to be a self-managed learner implies that courses need to require students to engage in independent learning. They will only become competent self-managed learners through practice.

> In the past couple of years, I emphasize more the enhancement of self-learning and arousing interest in students. For instance, we organize a case competition within the faculty. About 10 teams of roughly 100 students participate each year. We'll think of ways which make the competition a fun event. They are given a case on Friday and they have to present their analysis the next day. They will have to burn the midnight oil that night. They all moan but are fully charged and enjoy the whole event to the full, and they ask for more similar events. These kinds of activities are effective in motivating self-learning.
> (Gordon Cheung – CUHK – Management)

Competencies

Besides self-managed learning ability, the award-winning teachers cited a wide range of generic competencies which they felt their graduates should possess. There was variation in the competencies specified, but it is reasonable to claim that all felt that completing a degree meant more than acquiring knowledge of a discipline. A reasonably typical set of competencies is given in the quotation below.

> Our course is designed to help students develop their critical thinking and understanding, to be able to rationally appreciate, analyse, and intelligently debate any phenomena of the physical world. If our course prepares students in this way, our graduates will not only be professional engineers, they will also be educated citizens. They will be in a position to contribute to, and to be employed in, fields other than their own. They will have begun a life-long process of self exploration through their careers as professional engineers. If this is the case, I believe our students can truly be said to have had a tertiary education. We also assist students in developing skills in team work, leadership, decision-making, oral and written communication, and negotiation. I think our course will produce much better community members who'll have the technical skills and understanding to solve community problems.
> (Bob Lord – RMIT – Communication Engineering, B B & P, p. 320)

As countries strive to develop knowledge-based economies, these competencies are becoming even more important. Governments and employers have stressed the importance of graduates possessing generic competencies to enable them to cope with a future in which there will be few certainties and the relevance half-life of knowledge will decrease.

> Students nowadays do lack communication skills. Compared to students in the Western world, Hong Kong students are weaker in presenting their ideas. In the real world, it is very important to be able to articulate yourself. US students articulate very well in presentations. Even if they have inferior solutions, they can talk their way out. In the real world, it is very important to articulate verbally, in speech and in writing. . . . That's what troubles me the most. As an engineering teacher, I end up being an English teacher a lot of the time! Students may not realise that. I learned from real experience that English is more important than calculus skills in the engineering field, for example. I can say all of the above because I have obtained real-life experience in a company.
>
> (Soung Liew – CUHK – Information Engineering)

Developing these competencies is consistent with the teaching of the higher-order intellectual skills needed for a discipline. There is no need for courses dedicated to developing generic competencies as they should be developed through use within the context of the discipline. The best way to develop critical thinking is to make demands on students which require the practice of critical thinking.

> My approach to teaching History is to teach a way of thinking, a way of analysing material, a way of combining the empirical and the deductive to seek for truths while understanding there is no such thing as truth. I want my students to see the incredible complexity of human existence, past, present and future.
>
> (Leonora Ritter – Charles Sturt – History, B B & P, p. 24)

The development of capabilities is also consistent with the needs of professional programmes. Students need to develop a way of thinking about the types of ill-defined problems dealt with by the profession. They also need communication skills.

> First, you have to put yourself into patients' shoes; then use your professional knowledge to solve their problems. Patients usually come with some very vague complaints, such as, 'I have headache, or I have stomach ache'. You'll need to know how to ask questions and what kinds of examinations are needed. It's a doctor's responsibility to judge if their complaints are serious or not and treat them accordingly. Students tend to approach problems by memorising textbook knowledge, the 40 pages about headache, for example. Instead, they should

start from understanding the patient's situation, how they can ask the few questions so as to tease out that the symptoms are not related to the first ten cases, nor the last ten cases recorded in the books, and be left with only two possibilities, for instance.

(Gregory Cheng – CUHK – Medicine and Therapeutics)

Principle 4.1

Teaching and curriculum design needs to be consistent with meeting students' future needs. This implies the development of a range of generic capabilities including:

- self-managed learning ability,
- critical thinking,
- analytical skills,
- team-work,
- leadership, and
- communication skills.

Individual or group activity

What type of capabilities will be needed by graduates of the programme(s) you teach? Write out a list, which will then become part of the aims for the programme.

What is learning?

These aims have implications for what is understood by learning. Indeed the conception of learning understood by the award-winning teachers can be interpreted as an aim in itself. Many of the interviewees explained their interpretation of good teaching and learning.

Consistent with the aim of developing generic competencies was the idea that learning involved change. There was more to it than learning the knowledge associated with a subject.

> Learning is all about change. If there's no change, then no learning is going on. There are a whole lot of ways in which students can change. Sometimes what changes is their level of confidence, or their level of ability to communicate what they're thinking about. I don't have any particular criteria regarding which knowledge has to be gained. I guess

it depends on the individual student. Say a student comes in who will not speak in class and who has chosen to go right through their secondary career ducking eye contact with the teacher. If, at the end of semester, that student can stand up and talk to their peers about something they've been researching, that to me is as great an achievement as having a person come in with a fairly good level of academic knowledge and go out with an A.

(Wendy Crebbin – Ballarat – Education, B B & P, p. 146)

This meant that meaningful learning could involve discomfort. Chapter 5 introduces the principle that it is often necessary to challenge students' existing beliefs. This can be a difficult and painful experience.

Deep learning can be frustrating, uncomfortable and disconcerting for the learner, and it requires considerable explanation, encouragement, and justification by the teacher to help and reassure the learner through these uncomfortable moments.

(Bob Lord – RMIT – Communication Engineering, B B & P, p. 321)

What is teaching?

The idea of meaningful learning being disturbing is also inherent in the following quotation. The quotation starts by talking about good teaching but most of it deals with good learning. This is because a relationship is seen between teaching and learning, with the one functioning to facilitate the other.

Good teaching is whatever helps people to get good learning. And what is good learning? Good learning is immediate. It's fun. It enables you to become more powerful within whatever discourse you're operating in. I suspect good learning is also something that unsettles you so that you're no longer as sure as you were before. If you learn something and you say, 'Right, now I've got the answer', well, I don't really think that is good learning.

(Jo-Anne Reid – Deakin – Education, B B & P, p. 206)

This link between teaching and learning is explicitly made in the following quotation. The role is seen as that of a facilitator of learning.

I tell the students, 'I'm not here to teach you the English language, I'm here to help you learn it. I'm a supervisor of your learning, I'm a facilitator of your learning. I'm not your teacher'.

(Chamkaur Gill – Bond – English, B B & P, p. 6)

Principle 5. 1 is consistent with this belief about teaching because it stresses the importance of students being actively involved in learning activities. If it is accepted that teaching should be a process of facilitating student learning there are implications for the nature of the method of teaching adopted.

> Teaching matters less than student learning. I sometimes see academics confusing the two. Lecturing is the main teaching mechanism in higher education, and I believe it shouldn't be. Good teachers have to be good facilitators of learning strategies, not just experts in their field.
> (Mark Freeman – UTS – Economics and Finance, B B & P, p. 54)

The quotation below links facilitative teaching to the development of competencies. If students are intellectually challenged in their courses they are more likely to be prepared for challenges they meet in their eventual employment.

> My teaching is based very much on a belief, which I have found to be true in practice, that if you give students an opportunity to show initiative, to take risks, to be challenged, they will actually achieve a great deal more than you would normally expect of them. Then when they move on into their professional careers, they are better prepared to take risks.
> (Wendy Crebbin – Ballarat – Education, B B & P, p. 139)

The beliefs about teaching of the award-winners were student-centred and concerned with facilitating learning. There are other beliefs which are more teacher-centred and content-oriented. For a review of research into teachers' beliefs about teaching in higher education see:

Kember, D. (1997). A reconcepualisation of the research into university academics' conceptions of teaching. *Learning and Instruction, 7*(3), 255–275.

Are universities successful at nurturing capabilities?

Universities have traditionally thought of themselves as producing graduates well developed in higher-order thinking skills, such as critical thinking and problem-solving ability. However, there has been a growing body of criticism from governments, employers' bodies and even academics which suggests that graduates are often ill-equipped for the demands placed upon them in the workplace (for example Barrie, 2004; Daly, 1994; Hong Kong

Education Commission, 1999; Johnstone, 1994; Leckey and McGuigan, 1997; Longworth and Davies, 1996). The essence of much of the recent criticism is that the graduates lack the capabilities needed for a knowledge-based economy.

We have an activity we use in our course for teaching in higher education and for our professional development courses for teaching assistants which graphically demonstrates the effect of curriculum design and teaching on the way students learn and on learning outcomes. It also challenges any complacency about the ability of universities to develop graduate capabilities.

The activity examines approaches to learning, which were discussed by a number of the award-winning teachers (see quotations earlier in this chapter and in Chapters 5, 7 and 10). Approaches to learning have most commonly been characterised into deep and surface approaches (Marton and Säljö, 1976). Students may have a preferred or predominant approach, but will also choose the approach seen as most appropriate for a particular assessment task or the prevailing teaching and learning environment. The characteristics of deep and surface approaches are described below.

Deep approach

- A deep approach is adopted when the student is interested in the topic or the academic task.
- As a result there is an attempt to understand key concepts or the underlying meaning of an article.
- An attempt is made to relate together the concepts to make a coherent whole. A piece of writing will be logically related with an introduction and conclusion.
- New knowledge will be related to previous knowledge and to personal experiences.

Surface approach

- An activity or assignment is undertaken because it is a set task and the course cannot be passed unless the assignment is completed. The task does not arouse interest.
- As a result the minimum possible time and effort is devoted to the task.
- There is no attempt to reach understanding of key concepts, instead reliance is placed upon memorisation of model answers or key facts perceived as likely to appear in tests or examinations.
- Coherence of the topic is not sought; so material is seen as a set of unrelated facts.
- Concepts are not related to personal experience; so remain as abstract theory. As a result what has been memorised is normally quickly forgotten.

📖   A deep and comprehensive understanding of approaches to learning can be achieved by reading:

Marton, F., Hounsell, D. and Entwistle, N. (1984). *The experience of learning*. Edinburgh: Scottish Academic Press.

Measuring approaches to learning

The revised version of the Study Process Questionnaire (R-SPQ) gives a quick and convenient measure of deep and surface approaches to learning (Biggs et al., 2001). A copy of the R-SPQ is shown in Box 4.1.

Box 4.1 Revised Study Process Questionnaire

Please choose the *one* most appropriate response to each question by filling in the appropriate circle alongside the question number. The numbers alongside each question stand for the following responses.

1 – this item is *never or only rarely* true of me
2 – this item is *sometimes* true of me
3 – this item is true of me about *half the time*
4 – this item is *frequently* true of me
5 – this item is *always* or *almost always* true of me

1. I find that at times studying gives me a feeling of deep personal satisfaction.   ① ② ③ ④ ⑤

2. I find that I have to do enough work on a topic so that I can form my own conclusions before I am satisfied.   ① ② ③ ④ ⑤

3. My aim is to pass the course while doing as little work as possible.   ① ② ③ ④ ⑤

4. I only study seriously what's given out in class or in the course outlines.   ① ② ③ ④ ⑤

5. I feel that virtually any topic can be highly interesting once I get into it.   ① ② ③ ④ ⑤

6. I find most new topics interesting and often spend extra time trying to obtain more information about them.   ① ② ③ ④ ⑤

7. I do not find my course very interesting so I keep my work to the minimum.   ① ② ③ ④ ⑤

8. I learn some things by rote, going over and over them until I know them by heart even if I do not understand them.   ① ② ③ ④ ⑤

9. I find that studying academic topics can at times be as exciting as a good novel or movie.   ① ② ③ ④ ⑤

10. I test myself on important topics until I understand them completely.   ① ② ③ ④ ⑤

11. I find I can get by in most assessments by memorising key sections rather than trying to understand them.   ① ② ③ ④ ⑤

12. I generally restrict my study to what is specifically set as I think it is unnecessary to do anything extra.   ① ② ③ ④ ⑤

13. I work hard at my studies because I find the material interesting.   ① ② ③ ④ ⑤

14. I spend a lot of my free time finding out more about interesting topics which have been discussed in different classes.   ① ② ③ ④ ⑤

15. I find it is not helpful to study topics in depth. It confuses and wastes time, when all you need is a passing acquaintance with topics.   ① ② ③ ④ ⑤

16. I believe that lecturers shouldn't expect students to spend significant amounts of time studying material everyone knows won't be examined.   ① ② ③ ④ ⑤

17. I come to most classes with questions in mind that I want answering.   ① ② ③ ④ ⑤

18. I make a point of looking at most of the suggested readings that go with the lectures.   ① ② ③ ④ ⑤

19. I see no point in learning material which is not likely to be in the examination.   ① ② ③ ④ ⑤

20. I find the best way to pass examinations is to try to remember answers to likely questions.   ① ② ③ ④ ⑤

Group activity

In our workshops and course for teaching in higher education we give each participant two copies of the R-SPQ and ask each to complete the questionnaire twice.

1. The first time is for either how they study now or how they studied in their favourite university course. Many of the participants are taking higher degrees so they normally find it easiest to refer to studying for that.
2. The second time is for how they studied in the course they disliked most at university. This was usually a compulsory course they did not want to take. The subject was not of great interest and the teaching was poor.

Having completed the two copies of the questionnaire each participant works out a score for deep and surface approaches (DA and SA) for their favourite and most disliked courses. Half of the items on the questionnaire measure the extent of use of a deep approach and the other half a surface approach. Deep and surface approach scores are then worked out simply by adding the scores for each item contributing to that approach. The score is the number in the circle filled in or ticked. For example a response of 'this item is *sometimes* true of me' has a score of 2.

Favourite course

DA = score for items 1 + 2 + 5 + 6 + 9 + 10 + 13 + 14 + 17 + 18
DA = $\ominus$ + $\ominus$ + $\ominus$ + $\ominus$ + $\ominus$ + $\ominus$ + $\ominus$ + $\ominus$ + $\ominus$ + $\ominus$ =
SA = score for items 3 + 4 + 7 + 8 + 11 + 12 + 15 + 16 + 19 + 20
SA = $\ominus$ + $\ominus$ + $\ominus$ + $\ominus$ + $\ominus$ + $\ominus$ + $\ominus$ + $\ominus$ + $\ominus$ + $\ominus$ =

Most disliked course

DA = score for items 1 + 2 + 5 + 6 + 9 + 10 + 13 + 14 + 17 + 18
DA = $\ominus$ + $\ominus$ + $\ominus$ + $\ominus$ + $\ominus$ + $\ominus$ + $\ominus$ + $\ominus$ + $\ominus$ + $\ominus$ =
SA = score for items 3 + 4 + 7 + 8 + 11 + 12 + 15 + 16 + 19 + 20
SA = $\ominus$ + $\ominus$ + $\ominus$ + $\ominus$ + $\ominus$ + $\ominus$ + $\ominus$ + $\ominus$ + $\ominus$ + $\ominus$ =

The scoring key for the R-SPQ can be downloaded at
http://www.routledge.com/textbooks/9780415420259.

Individual activity

When we run the activity with the R-SPQ we ask participants to write their scores for deep and surface approaches, in their favourite and most disliked courses, in a table on a whiteboard. Below are ten typical scores taken from participants in one of the courses.

Imagine you are a facilitator for the course. How would you debrief the activity? What lessons do you think can be learnt from these data?

Favourite course		Most disliked course	
DA	SA	DA	SA
39	25	31	34
36	28	16	50
37	*19*	*36*	*20*
45	14	22	25
45	19	16	41
37	*20*	*36*	*31*
39	23	18	40
38	28	18	35
38	20	23	38
39	16	16	47

Influence of teaching and learning environment on approaches to learning

Perhaps the most striking feature of the above R-SPQ data is the distinction between the approaches to learning in the favourite courses and those in the most disliked courses. Deep approach scores in the favourite courses are quite high and surface approach scores lower. This is quite predictable. Future university teachers and instructors surely have an interest in their subject and try to understand concepts.

In most cases the scores for the most disliked course are markedly different. The typical pattern is for the deep approach score to fall and the surface approach score to rise, often by substantial amounts. The implication here is that the teaching, the curriculum design and the nature of the teaching and learning environment can make a very marked difference to students' approaches to learning and learning outcomes. These were model students, yet most remembered at least one course where their approach to learning was far from the ideal.

This is a very salient lesson for all teachers. The way you teach and the design of your courses will have a definite impact on the way your students learn. Following the lessons learnt from the award-winning teachers will encourage the type of approach to learning displayed in favourite courses.

Individual variation

As well as the marked influence of the learning context, the data also show individual variation. There are always variations in learning approaches between individuals studying the same course. There will be an overall effect, but there will be differing starting points and not everyone will be affected equally.

Different reactions to favourite and least favourite courses can also be seen in the data above. The most common pattern is for deep approach scores to decline and surface approach scores to rise in the most disliked course, normally by substantial amounts. The third set of scores in the table above has almost identical scores for favourite and most disliked course. Most groups doing this activity have one participant like this – the highly conscientious student who studies in a model way however boring the course or however poor the teaching. Notice also the sixth set of scores. This participant has almost the same deep approach score in both types of course, but a much higher surface approach score in the most disliked course. This pattern of scores has also been common. It indicates a student who prefers to use a deep approach but needs to memorise material because that is what the assessment demands.

The degree of individual variation shows another reason for the importance of Principle 6.2, which stresses the need to get to know students as individuals. Students do not learn the same way or respond to particular teaching in the same way. Good teachers try to cater for individual differences as much as possible, though class size does impose obvious restrictions on this.

Effect of university teaching on deep approach

The way in which approaches to learning is affected by university teaching is worth examining because it is related to the development of the capabilities discussed earlier in this chapter. If students employ a surface approach there is little likelihood of them developing higher order thinking capabilities such as critical and creative thinking. Use of a deep approach can be seen as a precursor to the nurturing of such capabilities.

Figure 4.1 shows deep approach scores by year of study gathered from a sample of 4,863 students from over half of the departments in one university in Hong Kong. The data were gathered with the original version of the SPQ;

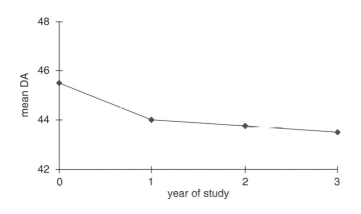

Figure 4.1

so the scores are not comparable to those above, but the meaning is the same. Year zero is when students enter the programme, while year three data were gathered at the completion of the final year of their degree.

The data show that as students proceeded through their programme their interest declines and they became less inclined to try to understand material. Unfortunately this is not just the effect of one atypical university. A similar finding seems to occur whenever a large sample of SPQ data has been gathered from across a range of departments (e.g. Biggs, 1987, 1992; Gow and Kember, 1990; Watkins and Hattie, 1985). It appears to be quite normal for universities to demotivate their students and encourage them to use less desirable approaches to learning as they proceed through their programme.

The reports cited earlier of graduates without sufficiently developed capabilities can now be understood. If universities are not encouraging students to employ a deep approach, neither are they doing a great deal to nurture higher order intellectual qualities like critical thinking.

A more encouraging example

Fortunately the outcome depicted in Figure 4.1 does not always occur. There are examples from more restricted samples, such as single programmes or degrees, for which deep approach scores rise by year of study.

A good example is shown in Figure 4.2 taken from SPQ data from four successive intakes to a radiography department (Kember and McKay, 1996; McKay and Kember, 1997). Intakes RPD1 and RPD2 were the final two cohorts for a Professional Diploma in Radiography. Their SPQ data show a similar pattern of declining scores to the graph above.

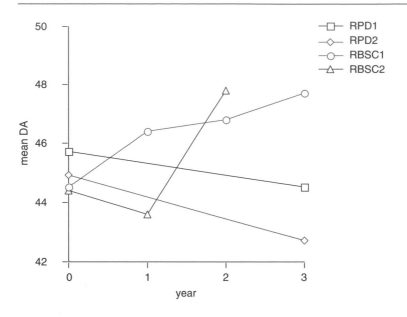

Figure 4.2

The department wished to upgrade its offering to a BSc degree. For purposes of external accreditation the curriculum had to undergo major changes and the staff of the department engaged in staff development activities for teaching and curriculum development. The revised course shifted away from the content-centred didactically taught diploma to more student-centred teaching. The number of hours of lectures was reduced significantly and students spent more time on self-directed learning and activities such as projects. More details about the changes to the curriculum are given in Kember and McKay (1996) and McKay and Kember (1997). Essentially, the teaching and learning moved closer to the principles developed in this book.

Chapter 5

What to teach

Fundamental concepts

This chapter derives some principles which apply to the selection of content. These are applicable when planning courses, writing lecture notes or preparing seminars and tutorials.

The first principle provides a guide for what to focus on when teaching. The award-winning teachers were clear that their teaching concentrated upon ensuring that their students developed a thorough understanding of key concepts which were fundamental to their discipline. A rationale for this principle was presented through an analogy to trees in a jungle. Understanding key concepts enables students to navigate the thick tangle of presented material. Without a set of key coordinates it is easy to get lost in the jungle.

> I believe that as statisticians, students need to understand some concepts before they are presented with some key arguments. It is like giving them a whole picture of the landscape of the jungle before going into details with a particular tree so that they won't get lost in the jungle right at the start.
>
> (Fan Jianqing – CUHK   Statistics)

A further rationale for aiming to ensure that students understand fundamental concepts is that these are often precursors to being able to grasp the remaining material. Students need a framework of fundamental points before they can build a body of knowledge.

> Discipline experts understand the material in a certain way, but I think an expert educator understands the material in a way that is a little different. An educator identifies the sticking points (the difficult concepts). For example, I had taught FM a few times and I kept getting ridiculous answers back from the students and I couldn't work out why, and then suddenly I realised there was one concept they weren't understanding.

So I introduced an analogy to help them grasp the concept and the problem didn't recur to the same extent. To do this, I had to cut back on time spent on some of the other content, but overall their understanding improved because the focus was on what they needed most to understand. Now I simply apply this principle all the time, and this is how the balance of the course is worked out.

(Bob Lord – RMIT – Communication Engineering, B B & P, p. 326)

Concentrating upon fundamental concepts may mean sacrificing some coverage. There is a justification for doing so in that students will learn little of the secondary material unless they have a thorough understanding of the key concepts which underpin them.

My colleagues in the profession expect me to teach a huge amount of content, but I think it's far more important that I teach students to learn. Don't get me wrong: some of this content is important, and I think we should cover enough content that we don't become negligent. But because the world is changing so quickly, we should give students at least a few frameworks and approaches that will enable them to deal with new information as they receive it and to apply concepts to new problems as they encounter them. I want students to really understand the concepts that I'm teaching and I think I'm starting to succeed in this.

(Mark Freeman – UTS – Economics and Finance, B B & P, p. 47)

There are some who feel that covering a large body of content establishes the credibility of their course. However, teaching a lot of material does not imply that students will learn a lot. Teaching more and more normally results in less and less learning. Surely it is the amount which is learnt rather than how much is covered which is important.

My teaching is not content-driven. I teach how to solve problems. Some students will panic after my class, 'When teaching lymphatic lumps, you've only taught two ways of solving the lymphatic problems. But there are 14 different types and you haven't even mentioned them! What can we do if they come up in exams?'

I'll explain to them that they can find the details of the 14 types in the textbooks, which will have much better detail than I can ever cover in a lesson. For me to repeat these facts in class is meaningless. The specific details of the 14 types are not necessary unless they become specialists in this field. The most important at this stage is for them to be able to distinguish the serious from the not-serious cases, and what further steps need to be taken to help the patient.

(Gregory Cheng – CUHK – Medicine and Therapeutics)

Even if a material is learnt, it is not necessarily remembered for long. One of the interviewees was willing to admit that she remembered little about a major area of law after finishing her course. If those who end up as professors can forget so quickly, the average student is likely to remember even less. This provides a further justification for concentrating on the fundamentals rather than the detail.

> Much of what students learn during their course will be obsolete by the time they graduate so there's no point in having them memorise a whole system of rules. That's just crazy. Besides, in six months' time most students will have forgotten the various rules of Law that we teach them here. I believe I was a very good Law student, and yet a year after I finished my course I could remember nothing about Company Law. Rather than concentrating on the rules of Law, I'm now trying to instil in them a deeper understanding, a deeper level of learning, and that makes the learning process a little slower. My students may not be given as much information as I was given, but they will have a deeper conceptual understanding. A student who understands the rule and why it is effectual or ineffectual will be able to give me the rationale. So even if the rule is missing, an understanding of the principle is there.
> (Marlene Le Brun – Griffith – Law, B B & P, pp. 416–417)

Even in subjects with a very rapidly changing knowledge base, such as computer engineering, fundamental concepts are still important. In some ways concentrating on them is more justifiable since the relevance half-life of recent advances is so short.

> In the field of engineering, the fundamental knowledge is most important, such as maths and programming. Technology advances rapidly while the fundamental knowledge remains unchanged. For example, Java has been popular for a while. Then a few months ago, Microsoft announced that they were not going to support Java anymore. That's why we teach the fundamentals so that students can establish a solid foundation and be able to adapt and learn new things more easily.
> (John Lui – CUHK – Computer Science and Engineering)

The stories from the award-winning Hong Kong teachers were comprehensive records of the interviews. It was, therefore, possible to see how many interviewees mentioned a particular principle. Another verification step was to send copies of the results of the analysis to the interviewed award-winning teachers to see if the interpretation was consistent with their beliefs. The importance of concentrating upon fundamental concepts was stated by 15 of the 18 interviewees. There was no disagreement with the analysis.

Principle 5.1

Ensure that students have a thorough understanding of fundamental concepts, if necessary at the expense of covering excessive content.

Relevance

The second principle related to what is taught was concerned with relevance. The award-winning teachers recognised that students are not motivated to learn abstract theory which appears to have no application. They need to perceive a clear rationale for why a topic is included in the syllabus. Three ways of establishing relevance were explained in the interviews.

To real life

The following quotation provides a rationale for ensuring that students can see the relevance of what is taught. They are more likely to be motivated to understand and learn it. This is particularly important in subjects which are often considered theoretical or abstract. Mathematics and theoretical physics are good examples.

> It gives me a buzz when I can relate the abstract to the practical or real world situations. I also find that students tend to be far more sympathetic to the learning process if they can match the abstract to the practical. In other words, they can see some way of touching the world around them by using abstract mathematics or computing or whatever they're involved in. Rather than just give the formal mathematics to them, I tend to say, 'Well, let's see – how the hell do you use this? What do you do with it?'. Even at fourth year level, where I teach very abstract units in theoretical physics, I still insist that they be able to calculate something that relates to the real world at the end of it. And some students find it absolutely amazing that this stuff actually does have something to do with the real world.
>
> (Michael Morgan – Monash – Physics, B B & P, p. 262)

Another subject which is often taught in a purely theoretical way is statistics. It does not have to be taught that way though. Relevant examples bring the subject to life.

> Let me give a very simple statistics example – hypothesis testing. It is a little bit dry and people don't understand it very well. I will explain it using a real-life situation such as drugs use in health service. Doctors

may not be able to judge if certain drugs are effective or not since there are variations in usage among the health care population in which some doctors will prescribe them to patients and some don't. Results show that there are small differences. How do we know if the differences are by chance, or intrinsically, one drug is better than the other? This is an elementary enough example. But you can make it even more elementary. People think that they can tell the difference between Coke and Pepsi. So I bring the drinks in without labels and ask them to taste and tell me which is which. If 50% of the answer is correct, it is quite obvious that they guess it right by chance. What about 55% and more? The question then is, where is the cut-off point that we can confidently say that you have the ability to differentiate between Coke and Pepsi?

So these are very simple, concrete real-life examples to stimulate students' interest in learning and make important concepts more easily understood. After that, we can go into more detailed, abstract and complicated examples.

(Fan Jianqing – CUHK – Statistics)

To current issues

Another way of showing relevance is to use examples currently in the news. This way of establishing relevance tends to be more applicable to some subjects than others, but most teachers could find something in the news which relates to their subject.

Keep asking them questions. Those are not technical questions that appear in textbooks. They are questions that emphasise everyday application. This is particularly important in business. . . . I myself have to watch the news twice a day and read a couple of newspapers to keep up to date with events which can be applied in management and then share them with students.

(Gordon Cheung – CUHK – Management)

To local examples

The third way of establishing relevance is to use local examples.

I try to make the teaching materials as relevant as possible to local situation. I use a lot of examples. For example, I refer to local cases such as Hong Kong mortgages. How do you compute interest statements? Students feel that these questions are real and practical.

(Zhang Shuzhong – CUHK – Operations Research)

The use of local examples is particularly important when the textbook originates in another country, as it often does. Anyone who has lived in a tropical climate will relate to the following example. Western textbooks give examples about heating a house, which is the last thing you need in a tropical summer.

> For example, it's very hot at the time of year when we hold these classes. I recall students talking with one mother about how she looks after her house, and she was talking about needing to keep cool. The American texts we use don't mention the difficulties of living in a climate like Townsville's and being eight months pregnant and feeling hot and uncomfortable all the time.
>
> (Justine Alison – James Cook – Nursing, B B & P, p. 358)

Principle 5.2

Establish the relevance of what is taught by:

- using real-life examples,
- drawing cases from current issues,
- giving local examples, and
- relating theory to practice.

Meshing theory and practice

Related to the need for relevance is relating theory to practice. This was the most frequently raised concern from those teaching professional courses. There was recognition that theory and practice needed to be integrated, but this was often not achieved.

> I have many concerns about how we teach the theoretical base of our discipline. In fact, I think many academic courses fail to integrate theory and practice. They either fail to teach theory at all or they teach theory in isolation from practice and then students have a terrible time when they go out into practice. They can rattle off the theory to you but they have trouble applying it. I think theoretical thinking is an absolutely foundational tool to be applied in any situation.
>
> (Pauline Meemeduma – James Cook – Social Work, B B & P, p. 118)

Many professional disciplines include periods students spend in practice. These are times when failures to integrate theory and practice can be cruelly exposed. Idealistic theories taught in the classroom leave them ill-prepared for practice if they find that quite different skills are needed or practices are more down to earth.

> Internships can challenge students to struggle with the mismatch between theory and practice. For example, in their lectures students are introduced to notions of rational decision making or incremental decision making as a tool – the idea that policy making involves a process of exploring options and assessing the likely impact of those various options. They often find this isn't the way it works in practice!
> (Elaine Thompson   UNSW – Political Science, B B & P, p. 94)

Students need to learn the knowledge base or theory which underpins their intended profession. They also need to know how the professionals make use of that knowledge – what they actually do in professional practice.

> For me, learning Law is about learning the process of Law. In Offices we attempt to make the Law real for the students. We attempt to refer back to what lawyers do and what lawyers will be doing in the future. We want the students to understand that in order to be a good lawyer they need to think about learning in these respects. We also try to give students a firm understanding of how their study is relevant to their lives. It's not just something that they memorise and then leave behind – it has some impact on who they are as informed citizens.
> (Marlene Le Brun – Griffith – Law, B B & P, p. 414)

Challenging beliefs

In the next chapter we will see that the award-winning teachers thought it was important to establish friendly relationships with their students. This did not, though, come at the expense of challenging students' preconceptions. Students can find confrontation of deep-seated beliefs a very disconcerting experience. However, if they are to get grips with fundamental concepts of a discipline challenging preconceptions is important.

> Paul Ramsden talks about 'deep learning'. I talk about my approach as 'tough learning'. I see learning as confronting what in some cases are very strongly held preconceptions. My kind of teaching is not just a process of adding on information, but rather it's a process of disrupting, of deliberately interfering with current ideas. At times I can actually see this happening – students literally squirm in their seats. The important thing at that point is to acknowledge and value the students' discomfort and to explain that this is a 'critical moment' of learning which is not to

be avoided. I'm actually quite passionate about it. I enjoy seeing people grappling with the material and being successful.

(Wendy Crebbin – Ballarat – Education, B B & P, p. 146)

The most fundamental beliefs which need to be challenged are the nature of learning and of knowledge. This was commonly observed for the Hong Kong students and their beliefs about knowledge are frequently found in other Asian students. The Hong Kong school system is highly competitive and examination-driven. To obtain a place at university students have to obtain high grades in the externally set examinations. Schooling sets a high priority on students' learning the examination syllabus, and remembering model answers is a common strategy. As a result of this conditioning at school, it is common for students to envisage learning as remembering material for examinations. Knowledge is something which is right or wrong. Multiple perspectives or conflicting theories have not been encountered. Such beliefs are clearly incompatible with university study, and so need to be challenged.

Unfortunately, in Hong Kong education, they are not trained to discuss and debate at primary and secondary levels. It's difficult for them to put down the old mode of learning and pick up discovery. . . . Students who grow up in Hong Kong, however, are generally frightened as they are so used to having model answers given to them in their secondary school training. 'You just give me the model answers, tell me all about the author and I will memorize, so that I can regurgitate during exams'. There were times when students were really frightened and dissatisfied with the fact that I had not given them the absolute model answers. So, it takes rather a long time to convince the students that the teacher is not there to tell me everything or hand down knowledge. It is I myself who need to think independently, analyse, discover and eventually understand.

(Lo Wai Luen – CUHK – Chinese Literature)

The issue of epistemological beliefs is not unique to Asian students, though their beliefs may be more pronounced because of the conditioning of competitive examination-driven school systems. Western university students display a range of epistemological beliefs and many hold ones which are not appropriate for university study.

For a very readable account of the range of epistemological beliefs found in university students see:

Perry, W. G. (1988). Different worlds in the same classroom. In P. Ramsden (ed.), *Improving learning: New perspectives* (pp. 145–161). London: Kogan Page.

Research into epistemological beliefs and abilities to make reflective judgements, which shows surprisingly naïve beliefs in university students, can be found in:

King, P. M. and Kitchener, K. S. (1994). *Developing reflective judgement: Understanding and promoting intellectual growth and critical thinking in adolescents and adults.* San Francisco: Jossey-Bass.

The need to challenge beliefs about knowledge goes across the disciplines. Science is sometimes said to be relatively factual. This belief in itself is open to challenge though.

Many students think science is a matter of using well-established methods that are the proper way to do things. They don't realise that some scientist at some stage just decided to do things this way and could quite easily have decided on another way. Students need to recognise that science is much more up in the air, more open, fuzzy and messy than they had previously thought. They get this understanding both from the actual projects they do, which rarely work as well as they expect, and just from talking to us and spending a week living with a bunch of people who are actually doing science.

(Alan Butler – Adelaide – Zoology, B B & P, p. 283)

📖 There is an extensive literature on conceptions and mis-conceptions in science education. Useful discussions can be found in:

Driver, R. and Erickson, G. (1983). Theories-in-action: Some theoretical and empirical issues in the study of students' conceptual frameworks. *Studies in Science Education*, *10*, 37–60.
Helm, H. and Novak, J. D. (1983). *Misconceptions in science and mathematics*. Ithaca, New York: Cornell University.
McDermott, L. C. (1984). Research on conceptual understanding in mechanics. *Physics Today*, *37*, July, 24–32.
Osborne, R. J. and Wittrock, M. C. (1983). Learning science: a generative process. *Science Education*, 67(4), 489–508.
West, L. H. T. and Pines, A. L. (eds) (1985). *Cognitive structure and conceptual change*. New York: Academic Press.

Engineering is also not seen as a factual subject. It is only by dealing with ill-defined problems that students can develop the reflective judgemental skills necessary for dealing with the type of messy problems that engineers and other professionals face in real life.

> Ability to think independently in an 'out of box' way. Not just 'problem set, solve the problem, compute the answers' which is a very typical way for engineering students. In real life, it is useful but not the most useful. What is important is to think independently, being able to solve an open-ended problem, finding answers by doing research, being able to articulate the trade-offs of different answers and weigh their pluses and minuses. In engineering, there are seldom right or wrong answers. There are always multiple possible answers. You have to weigh what is the trade-off of different solutions and try the best one for that particular situation. So, being able to adapt to the environment and find solutions in a very flexible way is important. That comes with communication skills.
>
> (Soung Liew – CUHK – Information Engineering)

Unlearning is frequently necessary in technical subjects. There are two reasons for this. One is the need to change beliefs about learning discussed above. The other is that students often hold inappropriate or out-dated conceptions of fundamental concepts. Unless they go through an often difficult process of conceptual change, they will have a shaky foundation of fundamental concepts on which to build other knowledge.

In this subject, a lot of unlearning also takes place. The students are used to a certain pattern of learning in their technical subjects where they study to pass exams rather than to develop critical and reflective understanding of the subject area. My subject therefore demands much 'unlearning' which the students find hard initially. Unlearning of misconceptions in Mathematics, unlearning of the way we learn. It's a difficult process that requires intensive support and encouragement from staff. Some students do begin to differentiate between meaningful learning and studying for marks. However, this recognition is not easily translatable into better learning practice in an overloaded course structure such as theirs.

(Keiko Yasukawa – UTS – Mathematics, B B & P, p. 306)

Principle 5.3

Challenging beliefs is important to:

- establish appropriate ways of learning and beliefs about knowledge, and
- deal with misconceptions of fundamental concepts.

Chapter 6

How to teach

Learning through doing

The first principle introduced in this chapter is that learning occurs through practice or practical application. The tenet is introduced here through an analogy to swimming, and the point is made that the same principle applies to learning a language. It also applies to all other subjects.

> Learning a language is like learning how to swim. No amount of theorising or standing by the pool watching others swim will help you become a swimmer. You can stand by the side and watch Kieren Perkins, and you can say, 'Hey, he's got great strokes, that's the right way to do it', but if you don't practise you're not going to be like him. Now language is essentially like this.
>
> (Chamkaur Gill – Bond – English, B B & P, p. 5)

The same case is argued in a more general way in the following quotation. Just listening to a teacher tends to result in surface learning. Understanding comes through active engagement. Teaching which is purely didactic is unlikely to result in a thorough understanding of key concepts.

> I believe very strongly that students only learn by doing – they must be intellectually engaged in the learning process. It is becoming increasingly obvious that traditional didactic exposition, no matter how well it is done, produces at best superficial learning. So I adopt a 'hands-on' (or 'brains-on') approach which promotes active learning on the part of the student. We have minimised the use of formal mathematics and we have developed a lot of software. The students do most of their learning in the laboratory and the lectures are there basically to signpost the main ideas. What's important is that they learn and master the ideas.
>
> (Michael Morgan – Monash – B B & P, Physics, p. 264)

The principle suggests that learning occurs more through what the students do than through what the teacher says. This relates to the discussion of the nature of teaching in Chapter 4. The award-winning teachers saw it as an important part of their teaching to orchestrate these student activities. How the principle was put into practice will be seen in Chapters 9 to 11.

Learning through discussion

Perhaps the most important form of active learning is discussion. Engaging in interactive dialogue means that students have to think actively about the key points under discussion. Good questioning techniques can show whether concepts have really been understood.

> I prefer to teach in an interactive 'question and answer' format. It is recognised in medical training that the lecture style of teaching is the least effective while direct interaction is considered the most effective. Prolonged interaction is preferred to allow students to review real cases and examples. We don't have that much one-way lecturing. If we do, it won't last longer than 30–40 minutes, whereas a continuous Q and A tutorial session can last for an hour and a half.
>
> (Leung Sing Fai – CUHK – Clinical Oncology)

If teaching is interactive it is also more flexible and adaptable to what happens in class. Dialogue with students provides a means of gauging whether concepts have been understood. If not, other approaches can be tried until they catch on.

> What makes good teaching? Well firstly, that you engage and keep the students' attention. I think there is something unique about human interaction. I like to look around the room and see whether there's somebody in the group who's not firing. If so, I go back and open things up, and talk to them about whatever it is they're not following, aiming to move their conceptualisation on the issue up a notch by the time they leave the lecture theatre. So good teaching isn't just the transfer of knowledge, it's the transfer of a conceptualisation. Keeping them interested, trying to say things in a way that engages them, is what I think makes good teaching.
>
> (Elaine Thompson – UNSW – Political Science, B B & P, p. 98)

Discussion through email

Face-to-face interaction is normally found to be better for establishing an initial rapport. Discussion through email and web forums is valuable once relationships are established. It can be good for promoting student–student dialogue. It can also be hard work for the teacher.

> I emphasise communications with students, particularly communications outside classroom teaching. In recent years, I have created a web forum for each class so that students can post questions whenever they need and wherever they are. And I'll respond as soon as possible. The forums are monitored several times a day, seven days a week. Meanwhile, I equally encourage students to come to me personally to ask questions and have face-to-face interaction.
>
> (Chu Ming Chung – CUHK – Physics)

For distance-education students electronic communication provides a vital channel for interaction, which is otherwise lacking.

> Distance-education students usually aren't able to benefit from the advantages of this physical environment, but in a computer-supported collaborative learning environment they can, to some extent, enjoy some interaction and some of the other 'goodies' of a face-to-face teaching environment.
>
> (Som Naidu – Southern Queensland – Education, B B & P, p. 185)

Principle 6.1

Meaningful learning is most likely to occur when students are actively engaged with a variety of learning tasks. Discussion is an important learning activity.

Building relationships with students

For there to be interaction between students and the teacher a rapport needs to be developed. As well as facilitating discussion, establishing harmonious teacher–student relationships can be a good motivating force.

> By projecting ourselves as genuine teachers, with empathy, we can build up a trustful relationship with students. This relationship is a key factor for enhancing the motivation of students. I would like students to have self motivation.
>
> (Patrick Lau – CUHK – Educational Psychology)

To establish a rapport the initiative needs to come from the teacher. Students are normally willing to respond, but it is hard for them to take the first step.

> I teach very personally. I practise very personally too. I think true human engagement is a real sharing of selves. It's not about a one-sided sharing by one person while the other gives very little. So when I teach and when I practise I talk about myself. I talk about what's happening to me, and I talk about all the things I get up to. I think that's part of my deliberate attempt to demystify academics.
> (Pauline Meemeduma – James Cook – Social Work, B B & P, p. 124)

It is not difficult to create the opposite impression – that you do not want to be bothered by students out of class. If teachers disappear as soon as a class ends and avoid students with queries they end up with more free time – but they will never become an award-winning teacher.

> Numerous Asian students have complained to me about their Australian teachers not being very sensitive about their concerns and being un-approachable. I've seen so many cases of teachers not making themselves available or finding excuses for not talking to the students. I think this drives a wedge between the student and the teacher. I gain my students' confidence by being a friend.
> (Chamkaur Gill – Bond – English, B B & P, p. 8)

Many Western universities now recruit overseas students; so many teachers have Asian students in their classes. Some find them rather reserved – less confident to speak out in class compared to local students. This is perhaps not surprising, given that all are in a foreign environment and many experienced school atmospheres more formal than most Western schools. In their home countries the ice can be broken and the CUHK exemplary teachers had all established close ties to their students. Those who teach overseas Asian students will find that they too can develop confidence in speaking up in class if they make an effort to build bridges. A good starting ploy is to use the techniques for prompting discussion in class described in Chapter 10.

> The relationship between teachers and students in Chinese society is usually hierarchical. Nowadays, young people are different from those in the old days. They expect a friendship-type of relationship between their teachers and themselves. Teachers have to adjust their attitude. Both teachers and students should communicate in a mutually accept-able attitude and should understand each other.
> (John Chi Kin Lee – CUHK – Curriculum and Instruction)

Interaction out of class

Availability out of class was a common characteristic of the award-winning teachers. Being available to answer queries encourages students to work outside class time. Though, if you prefer your office to yourself at times, availability needs to be managed.

> My office is like Central Station most of the time. My post-graduate students come to my home as well. There are always students in here, sharing what they've done out on prac or just talking about whatever they happen to be worried about. There have been times when our Head of Department has said that the students have to start making appointments through the secretary, but that never lasts more than a couple of days. I could put a notice on my door and say 'I don't want to be disturbed' but they'll laugh and knock anyway. It actually makes for a very exciting working environment. We see ourselves as a team. With the students everyone is a learner.
>
> (Dawn Francis – James Cook – Education, B B & P, p. 171)

Several of the interviewees described out-of-class activities which proved to be effective in establishing good teacher–student relationships.

> The camps achieve a number of positive outcomes. Firstly, they provide an opportunity for the students and staff to get to know each other before the in-semester grind begins. This generally improves student morale and the students get to recognise that the staff members are human beings and they can talk to staff freely. I think this carries over into their other subjects as well.
>
> (Alan Butler – Adelaide – Zoology, B B & P, p. 285)

Getting to know students

An important aspect of establishing good teacher–student relationships is getting to know students as individuals. It is much easier to build a bridge to an individual you know than to a sea of faces.

> I strongly believe that a good lecturer, a good teacher, combines the caring humanistic qualities with good academic rigour. I suppose that's very much a driving force and cooperative learning serves me well in providing this balance. I believe a good relationship between teacher and learner is crucial for effective learning, at any level of education. I try as much as possible to get to know individual students, to communicate that I care for the student as an individual.
>
> (Toni Noble – ACU – Educational Psychology, B B & P, p. 224)

Learning names is important. It is also valuable to find out something about the students. Getting to know each other may take time out of the first class – but this is time well spent.

> In the first week of the semester, my aim is for them to come out knowing everybody's name in the group and something about everybody in the group. I work really hard in those first three hours to break down the nervousness and help them get to know each other.
>
> (Dawn Francis – James Cook – Education, B B & P, p. 165)

Remembering names is not easy if your memory is as poor as mine (DK). I ask students to wear name-tags for the first few classes. Francis Chan uses a more imaginative technique.

> One technique that I use to break the ice and gradually warm students up for active learning is to remember students' names. In a group of 15 students, they will introduce their names which are impossible for me to remember them all instantly. So I'll joke with them, 'I will only call on the ones whose names are easy to remember.' They'll start laughing. 'Those who have got easy names, if you don't want me to call on you all the time, you had better give me other fellow students' names after I have asked the question.'
>
> (Francis Chan – CUHK – Medicine and Therapeutics)

Getting to know part-time students is particularly important. Part-time study is far from easy and an empathetic teacher helps with the difficult task of balancing full-time work with part-time study. Good teachers also make use of the knowledge and expertise of their part-time students, as many of them are employed in positions related to the field they are studying. If you know what they do you can draw them into the class discussion.

> We teach a lot of part-time classes. Students work from nine to seven. They are tired when they go to the class. If you can't arouse their interest, they will be 'dead'. To stimulate their interest is basic but challenging. You have to find out who your students are, their concerns and what motivates them.
>
> (Andrew Chan – CUHK – Marketing)

Principle 6.2

Establishing empathetic relationships with students is a pre-requisite to successful interaction with them. To do this you need to know them as individuals.

Reflection

Do you know the names of the students in your class?
Do you know anything about them?
Unless your class is large, you should be able to answer yes to these questions by a few weeks into the semester. If you find remembering names difficult try some of the following:

- Take sticky labels along to class; so that your students can wear name tags.
- Ask each student to briefly introduce themself at the start of the first class.
- Ask each student to write a short description of themself on a card.
- Ask students to provide a photograph of themselves or take along a digital or Polaroid camera to the first class.

Chapter 7

Motivating students

Accepting responsibility for motivating students

Perhaps the most important point about motivating students comes right here at the beginning of the chapter. The award-winning teachers believed that it was their responsibility to motivate students. A vital part of the role of a teacher is to enthuse, inspire and motivate their students.

> I think one of the greatest skills an educator can have is the skill to inspire students, to motivate them, to get them excited. That's what I enjoy. I think you can stimulate their minds, enthuse them, send them on a quest for learning. I think we do, in a way, send them off on a voyage of discovery to broaden their knowledge and open new doors.
> (Lindsay Johnston – Newcastle – Architecture, B B & P, p. 444)

Such views are not universal. A 'blame the student' mentality is common. Adherents to this belief feel that students should be motivated to learn however dull, irrelevant and uninspiring their teaching and courses. This view was not consistent with the beliefs of the award-winning teachers. Every single one of the CUHK interviews made some mention of the need to motivate students, and it was a common theme in the Australian interviews.

> By the end of the semester I want students to be thinking of learning as a terrific adventure. I want them to gain a certain amount of knowledge as part of this adventure and to know how to apply that knowledge. I want them to know how to ask questions and how to see patterns. I want them to know where they can go to find things out. I want my students to leave being good historians.
> (Leonora Ritter – Charles Sturt – History, B B & P, p. 21)

Having high expectations

The award-winning teachers needed to motivate their students because they had high expectations of them. Their courses were demanding and they were prepared to push their students towards their exacting targets.

> Generation after generation of students know that I'm tricky, fierce, fastidious and I make them work a lot. Right from the very first lesson, I will tell them very clearly my expectations and requirements. I will have given them the course outlines and references. Also, I'll tell them that they can reselect modules after the first week and, if they prefer not to change, they should not regret ever choosing my subjects. They consciously know what to expect.
>
> (Lo Wai Luen – CUHK – Chinese Literature)

One of the toughest aspects of their courses occurred when beliefs were challenged. As was explained in Chapter 5, confronting established beliefs was necessary in order to establish beliefs about knowledge suited to higher education or to form proper interpretations of key concepts.

> My course is not easy – it's really quite challenging for students and sometimes disturbing too. Students become aware of the real extent of problems in the world and their own levels of response to these problems. I've had students withdraw from my courses – not many, but a few – who just simply found things too confronting. I guess part of an academic's responsibility is to know how far you can push a student, and I think that often in the university system, particularly in some of the social sciences, we really set out to destabilise people's beliefs and that's not good. I think you can push people in a gentle way, in a reflective way and challenge them, but undertaking a full scale demolition of their beliefs is not a good thing to be doing.
>
> (Jim McKnight – UWS – Psychology, B B & P, p. 243)

Having demanding requirements of students was a common expectation as 11 of the 18 CUHK interviewees explicitly mentioned them. In addition, the three teachers from the medical faculty said their integrated curriculum placed heavy demands on students.

The demands made on students need to be challenging but reasonable. Excessive workload tends to promote a surface approach to learning as students cut corners to cope with overwhelming demands. Greater demands can be made if the curriculum is interesting and student-centred learning approaches are employed (Kember, 2004). Dawn Francis captured the essence of the reasonable position with the notion of a 'warm demander'.

I like the notion of being a 'warm demander'. I'm fairly relaxed and laid back in my teaching but I also make it very clear to students on the first day that I'm demanding. I'm passionate about my teaching and I expect them to be too. I usually get some laughter when I say I'm laid back and may seem very casual but in fact I'm very demanding and sometimes dictatorial. They all think that's hilariously funny.

(Dawn Francis – James Cook   Education, B B & P, p. 173)

When making demands on students make use of what you have learnt about their individual capacity and character. Students vary a great deal. Some can be pushed further than others. Some respond better to cajoling, some to praise and there are a few who respond most to threats.

You can be very tough. If they feel that they have learnt something, they appreciate it more. It's just like raising kids. You have to push your students to a limit. Some may like it, some may not. Different students may have different limits. You have to push them according to their own characters and personal limits.

(Soung Liew – CUHK – Information Engineering)

Before leaving the topic of making demands, we need to deal with the contrary view. There are those who believe that students pick the easiest courses and give high evaluation ratings to those teachers who make limited demands. There are undoubtedly some students who take this line, but the award-winning teachers thought they were a minority and certainly did not allow this perspective to influence their teaching.

What students complain about most is courses that are 'flat' ('tui', a slang word in Cantonese) which means that the lecturer is lazy, unenthusiastic and that the course exams are made easy to pass. Paradoxically to what you may have heard from students that they opt for easy courses, they actually despise courses which they feel are 'flat' and meaningless. They won't treat these courses seriously and degrade them into just 'getting a few credits'.

(Chu Ming Chung – CUHK – Physics)

Encouraging students

Having established that the award-winning teachers accepted responsibility for motivating students and had high expectations of them, we now need to see how they motivate students. The first strategy is encouraging students. When students meet the high demands they should be told that they have done so.

This is how I motivate my students: encourage them. If your boss or the VC comes and tells you, 'Good job! Good job!' I'm sure you'll do more. In contrast, if they say, 'You are not good enough . . .' you'll be demoralized.

(John Lui – CUHK – Computer Science and Engineering)

If students realise that a course is challenging, yet are sufficiently interested to achieve the aims, they will end up with a sense of accomplishment.

Effective teaching refers to arousing students' interests, inspiring them to deep learning, getting them interested in what is being taught and resulting in students having a sense of accomplishment in that learning has taken place within them. In my course, students can apply what they've learnt in situations outside the classroom. One common comment from my student course evaluations is: 'I am inspired'.

(Kenneth Leung – CUHK – Journalism)

Enthusiasm of the teacher

The next way of motivating students was through their own enthusiasm as a teacher and for their subject.

But above all, it's somebody who can convey the enthusiasm that they themselves feel to make the subject matter interesting.

(Gordon Mathews – CUHK – Anthropology)

Displaying enthusiasm as a teacher does not mean that the teacher has to put on a performance. This is discussed further in the next section. Conveying a passion for their discipline was the key element of enthusiasm displayed. Others should be able to display enthusiasm because it would be unusual to become an academic without having a fascination for one's discipline. Displaying enthusiasm means revealing to students your own interest in your discipline.

Looking back to my own experience as a learner, the teachers who really helped me were the ones who obviously were in love with teaching and were in love with the material that they taught. These teachers had many different styles. They weren't all up front, open wide, outgoing types of people but they all had that same passion for what they were teaching. They had a way of conveying a love of learning, a love of knowledge that was very infectious. They all had that excitement that conveyed to the student that this subject was worth knowing about. Most of the subjects that they taught me I don't have any dealing with anymore. I make very little use of geography. I make very little

use of French. I make very little use, I'm sad to say, of English Literature although I make some use of it. But I've never lost the feeling that
those subjects were worthy and interesting and that's something that
has led me to see that other subjects could be as well.

(Damian Conway – Monash – Computer Science, B B & P, p. 345)

As we saw in the previous chapter, it was also important to display sufficient interest in students to get to know them and establish a positive relationship with them.

Good teachers care passionately about both their subject and their
students. It's not enough to care passionately about your subject and
not give a damn about your students. That doesn't work because
students have to feel that they matter to you. Little things like trying to
remember their name are quite important. It makes the students feel
valued and gives them that sense of dignity. They've become a person
and not an object.

(Leonora Ritter – Charles Sturt – History, B B & P, p. 33)

Interesting and enjoyable classes

Both of the quotations in this section use the word 'boring'. Boring classes
are something to avoid.

You don't have to stand in the front and lecture sternly and show off
your knowledge to be a good teacher. A lot of this is pretty boring.
Teaching can be enjoyable and still you learn from it.

(Allan Walker – CUHK – Educational Administration)

To be a good teacher does not equate to being a good performer. There is
no doubt that some of the award-winning teachers were humorous or entertaining, but this is definitely not a condition of being a good teacher. The
research evidence suggests that when students give evaluation ratings they
are not swayed by the performers who put on a show (Marsh, 1987). If
you have a sense of humour use it. If you can think of entertaining anecdotes
utilise them. What is more important though is drawing on your own fascination with your discipline to make it interesting for your students. Few of
us are stand-up comedians or skilled actors, but we can aim to make lessons
interesting.

Good teaching is entertaining teaching. You'll hear some academics
say, 'We aren't here to entertain students'. I certainly think we are
here to entertain them! We're consuming two hours of their lives.
They're here to be entertained, not in the sense of razzamatazz but in

the sense of being engaged, in the sense that they find what you're offering interesting and they want to listen and want to find out more. One of the terrific things about case studies is that the students want to know the endings. They're not going anywhere until they find out what happened to Peter, for example. I think the cardinal sin of teaching is being boring. That annoys me no end. Poor teaching is boring teaching. (Pauline Meemeduma – James Cook – Social Work, B B & P, p. 128)

Relevant material

One of the principles derived in Chapter 5 was that students should perceive what is taught as relevant. Relevance could be established through real-life examples, local materials or current affairs. Establishing relevance in these ways makes a subject more interesting for students and motivates their learning.

> I try to make my lectures interesting and I bring in lots of examples and I try to use funny stories whenever I can. I use cartoons from the newspapers, still work drawings, anything that keeps the course lively.
>
> For example, a group decision-making exercise which is very well known. Recently, there was a good movie called 'Thirteen Days' which dealt with the US–Cuban missile crisis back in 1962. This movie has a sustained 20 to 25-minute segment in it that actually deals with the group decision-making process at the highest level of the US government in 1962. It is very interesting. Hollywood occasionally supplies us with all these beautifully designed films that are historically accurate. By and large, that movie comes right out of some of the transcripts that existed of the day. It is an effective combination of things.
>
> (David Ahlstrom – CUHK – Management)

A variety of active learning experiences

The final way to motivate students was to use a variety of teaching approaches involving active learning. Using the same teaching method for lesson after lesson becomes very tedious.

> The use of teaching methods depends on the objectives of that course, students' characteristics, needs and prior knowledge at various stages. You should not use the same one method throughout the whole course. Teaching methods vary from lesson to lesson. For the first lesson, I have to introduce myself and understand my students, their characters, needs and expectations. You cannot use the same approach

in Lesson 21! Add and remove different elements as you go along so
that your strategy fits in with the stage of development of your students.
(Andrew Chan – CUHK – Marketing)

Chapter 6 introduced the principle of learning through doing. The
rationale given was that students learn better if they actively engage with
the course material. A further reason for employing active learning methods
is that students find them more interesting and motivating.

> We can use the laboratory as part-lecture, part-tutorial, part-lab,
> part-informal discussion. We are able to have this interesting mix and
> interplay between the different types of teaching methodologies or
> pedagogies.
> (Michael Morgan – Monash – Physics, B B & P, p. 264)

Most active learning strategies involve interaction between students. This
can help develop a sense of belonging within a class, which is a further means
of motivation.

> Co-operative learning strategies create opportunities for students to
> quickly get to know and like each other and to enjoy being a class
> member. These strategies help to develop a sense of community among
> the students, even in a large lecture group. The variety of different
> co-operative learning practices serves to maintain student interest and
> engagement in learning.
> (Toni Noble   ACU – Educational Psychology, B B & P, p. 221)

Principle 7.1

Good teachers accept that it is their responsibility to motivate students
to achieve the high expectations they have of them. Motivation comes
through:

- encouraging students,
- the enthusiasm of the teacher,
- interesting and enjoyable classes,
- relevant material, and
- a variety of active learning approaches.

Part II

Principles into practice

Chapter 8

Planning courses and lessons

Course planning

This chapter is the first which concentrates on taking the principles, derived in the previous chapters, and shows how they can be put into effect. The chapter is about planning, and so relates strongly to Chapter 4 which dealt with aims. Principle 4.1 stressed the need for curriculum design to be consistent with meeting students' future needs.

Student needs

If these are to be met it is necessary to know enough about your students to anticipate their future needs. This means that curriculum plans cannot be set in concrete because future needs will change and the student body is changing. In some cases the change is progressive – often towards greater diversity. In other cases, as in the example below, there is variation between intakes.

> The student group changes continually. In the past, you could virtually guarantee the majority of students would be eighteen years old, highly intelligent, middle class. But now, the combinations change every year. Every year you get a new batch of students and every year it's a new deck of cards. Some years you're top heavy with mature-aged students. Other years you're top heavy with eighteen year olds who just giggle their way through life. You can never be complacent and say, 'Right, I've got this teaching package that I can slot in for the next five years'. At the end of the day, you have to pay attention to that living dynamic of learning/teaching exchange. You have to devise strategies that will bring about the most effective learning for those particular students. I like to get to know each group of students in order to address their learning needs.
> (Pauline Meemeduma – James Cook – Social Work, B B & P, p. 119)

This underlines the importance of Principle 6.2, though from a rather different perspective. Chapter 6 was about how to teach; so the principle was drawn upon to emphasise the need to know individual students in a class to develop an empathetic relationship. In the context of planning, the principle implies knowing enough about the characteristics of your student body to be able to anticipate their future needs in planning courses.

Determining the future needs of students means anticipating developments within the discipline or profession. As the pace of change in technology and society quickens, this is not a task to be underestimated.

> We don't stop at the 'here' and 'now'. We have to proactively think of the future trend of this subject five years down the line. Sometimes, things change so rapidly that we'll need to review and project to the future within three years, or even one year, as people's perceptions may have changed then.
>
> The expected level of student achievement in the subject ought to be clearly articulated. First of all, we must teach our students what these issues are. We must let them become aware of the future trends and what the appropriate approaches will be.
>
> (Andrew Chan – CUHK – Marketing)

An important element of students' future needs are the graduate capabilities incorporated into Principle 4.1. In the quotation below the planning looked at the values, skills and attitudes needed by future lawyers. There was also consideration given to more generic capabilities as law graduates often end up in fields other than law. As this commonly happens in other disciplines too, the need for programmes to nurture generic capabilities is underscored.

> When we designed this course we had a big brainstorm session. We thought about what lawyers do, what values they should hold, and what sort of skills they should have. We looked at the relationship between theories of Law and the skills, values and attitudes we felt would be appropriate for lawyers in the future. Then we decided which things would be appropriate for which years, and in which areas of law each of those skills would be best addressed. We looked at where Law graduates were going. The Graduate Careers Council of Australia indicates that after five years many, if not most, Law graduates aren't practising any more. This means we are not, and should not be, a professional training institute. I see Law as a generalist degree and I believe our curriculum needs to meet a fairly broad population need.
>
> (Marlene Le Brun – Griffith – Law, B B & P, p. 412)

In deciding the future needs of students the award-winning teachers did not peer into crystal balls; they took steps to gather useful information. This information could be gathered from alumni, those in the profession and incoming students. In the quotation below Andrew was talking about an MBA; so the students would all be working in the field and well aware of their own needs.

I collect such useful information by several means: I'll ask them to fill in a questionnaire 'What do you expect to learn in the course?'. Then I'll figure out what kinds of competencies are required of them from the real world. From time to time, I'll find out from alumni and business people what kinds of people are currently needed in their fields, and I will aim at developing such competencies in my students. Preceding that, I have to constantly update my literature understanding before designing the curriculum content. Therefore, the final curriculum content is tailored to meet current requirements and future trends alongside the understanding of prevailing issues in the academic world. I will integrate all this information and share with my students.

(Andrew Chan – CUHK – Marketing)

Individual or group activity

What are the future needs of students in the programme(s) you teach? Write a description to complete the set of aims for the programme.

Elements of curriculum planning

Planning the curriculum then involves a range of aspects. Firstly the aims need to be addressed. What are the important learning outcomes which need to be achieved if students' future needs are to be met?

The next aspect in curriculum planning is designing learning activities which will promote the achievement of these aims. Principle 6.1 observes that meaningful learning occurs through active engagement in learning tasks. Good curriculum planning includes designing learning activities which are consistent with the aims and intended learning outcomes.

The other element is the content of the programme. For much university teaching this is the only element of planning. Programme plans and course outlines commonly consist solely of lists of content topics. The award-winning teachers had a more holistic approach.

Course design is taken very seriously and carefully. At a programme level, the programme directors are responsible for identifying or selecting the most relevant courses. We ask ourselves:

- What are the objectives of the programme?
- What do we expect the graduates to achieve when they have completed the programme?
- What is required in the world and what are the future trends?

We will know what key areas are involved. For example, I am teaching marketing and I will focus on the needs and the trends in the arena of marketing. What is required of each of the different function areas in business education? In the process, you have to decide what academic purpose and what activities are desirable. We will design some basic elements for them together with some textbooks, exercises or case studies. Built-in learning activities are essential, such as inviting CEOs to give talks, visiting the PRC, helping them to establish their networks, arranging summer internships, offering free consultations to companies so students can gain solid work experience through their voluntary work, etc. I'll try to aggregate all the relevant elements, not only concentrating on text-based teaching.

To achieve this, you have to select the content and appropriate persons for the design and teaching of the course. Previous experience in teaching that particular subject is an important source of reference. We'll look into international practices for teaching approaches and materials.

(Andrew Chan – CUHK – Marketing)

This wider perspective on curriculum design does imply that more aspects are considered in the planning process. This may take a little more time, but the outcomes are worthwhile.

It's hard work to prepare for a new curriculum and to arrange a series of guest speakers. But I can tell from students' eyes that they really enjoyed it and were deeply moved. They were thankful for all these efforts: different input from different people with different voices.

(Lo Wai Luen – CUHK – Chinese Literature)

Structuring programmes

The traditional approach to curriculum design in universities has been the building-block approach. The foundation courses teach basic knowledge and subsequent courses build higher level knowledge on the foundations.

Finally, at the end of the degree, students get a chance to apply all this knowledge.

This building-block model is very logical, but it can also be very demotivating. Students spend course after course learning basic knowledge without any idea of its relevance to their selected discipline or profession. Exposing students to realistic open problems or projects earlier in a programme can help them to see why the basic knowledge needs to be in a course.

> Way back when I was a student, courses were designed such that you learnt all the basic things you needed to know, such as statistical techniques as well as current theory, as you went through. Then, after three years or so, you were ready to start applying all this knowledge. I don't believe that people actually learn as sequentially as that. People don't like learning things they may need some time in the future – they respond better if they discover the need by being unable to solve a problem, by making a mess of something. I put students in the position of having to do an experiment. When they try, they find they don't actually know how and they are motivated to want to learn. This is an oscillating sort of approach to education, not a sequential one.
>
> (Alan Butler – Adelaide – Zoology, B B & P, p. 279)

When considering the structuring of programmes it can also be worthwhile to take into account Principle 5.3 which says there may be a need to challenge beliefs about learning and knowledge. When students enter a programme believing that all questions have answers which are either right or wrong, activities and assessment might be planned so as to progress from relatively straightforward tasks at the outset to more open-ended ones as the programme progresses.

> So, my teaching will move from a more structured approach at the beginning to a more open-ended one towards the end; the teacher will move away from readily providing answers to giving no concrete answers eventually. This is exactly what the real world is: no definite answers for questions. At the start, they will gain confidence from 'getting the answers right'. This confidence is important to enable them to gradually discover that there are no absolute concrete answers, but rather a logic or framework of thinking, based upon which they can formulate their viewpoints, judgments and predictions. Learning is about developing their own thinking rather than finding model answers.
>
> (Andrew Chan – CUHK – Marketing)

Curriculum planning model

The aspects of curriculum planning can be incorporated into a model which shows how they relate together and influence each other. This model is shown in Figure 8.1.

At the top of the model are the student learning needs which were the starting point of Chapter 4. These lead to five elements of the curriculum which should be incorporated into curriculum plans; aims, fundamental concepts, learning activities, assessment and feedback. As we will see in Chapter 12, assessment has a very strong influence on learning outcomes. These are shown as related to student learning needs by a feedback loop to complete the cycle.

The central part of the model might be compared to the interaction model of curriculum development, one of those commonly cited in curriculum development texts (e.g. Brady, 1990). This consists of the four elements of objectives, content, activities and evaluation, with each element permitted to interact with each other.

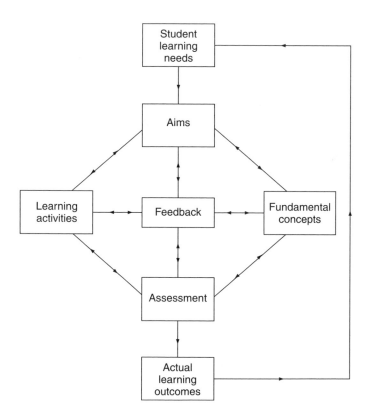

Figure 8.1

The curriculum model in Figure 8.1 uses the term aims, rather than objectives, mainly because the award-winning teachers commonly referred to high-level aims or goals, such as generic capabilities or learning to learn. However, there was very little mention of specific lesson-level objectives and no mention of behavioural objectives. In the courses we have run we have found that many academics find writing objectives difficult and not particularly helpful. If you are one of these then dispense with them, but make sure that degree- and course-level aims are taken into account in your planning. If you find writing more specific aims or objectives helpful in your planning, then use them.

Principle 5.1 is the reason the model refers to fundamental concepts rather than content. Considering fundamental concepts in planning courses gives consideration to desired learning outcomes, and so may be a substitute for objectives. Feedback is placed centrally within the other four curriculum elements to imply that feedback should be sought on all aspects of a curriculum and use made of it to iteratively fine-tune programmes and courses. Assessment is included as a separate element because Chapter 12 shows how strong its influence is on learning outcomes.

The five central elements are shown as linked and inter-related. In the interactive model of curriculum development the linking implies that the order of dealing with each element is not pre-determined. In our model the linking is intended to emphasise the importance of achieving consistency between the curriculum elements in the model. For a curriculum to succeed in achieving the intended learning outcomes each element needs to be related together in a coherent manner.

It is particularly important that the learning activities and assessment are consistent with the desired learning outcomes. If the student learning needs are the types of capabilities incorporated in Principle 4.1, the learning outcomes of at least some courses will need to involve the students in practising the desired skill. Critical thinking develops through students being engaged in critical discussion and writing. The ability to work in groups and communication skills are nurtured in group projects.

Principle 8.1

Planning programmes and courses involves consideration of students' future needs. The plans ensure that aims, fundamental concepts, learning activities and assessment are consistent with achieving outcomes related to future student needs. Feedback needs to be gathered to inform each of these elements in the curriculum design process.

Individual or group activity

Make a plan for a course you teach. Go beyond the typical university course outline, which often consists of little more than a brief list of content, by including elements from the curriculum development model. Use a table like that below, so that you can ensure that elements are consistent with each other.

Aims	Fundamental concepts	Learning activities

The course planning grid can be downloaded at http://www.routledge.com/textbooks/9780415420259.

Lesson planning

The model derived in the section above applies to programmes and courses. It will also inform the planning of lessons. By including the elements of aims, fundamental concepts, activities and assessment, plans will be more detailed than many university course outlines which contain little more than lists of content topics.

> Preparation is the secret of good teaching. I can't just go and teach off the top of my head. I've got to be confident in the subject I'm teaching, and I've got to be well prepared for it.
> (Justine Alison – James Cook – Nursing, B B & P, p. 362)

There is still work to do though before each lesson or class. The award-winning teachers recognised that thorough preparation is important to good teaching.

> First of all, good preparation is required on my part for each class. Without preparation, my teaching may become disorganized and confusing. I'll challenge myself, 'How can I explain the complex and difficult knowledge in the simplest ways?'
> (Francis Chan – CUHK – Medicine and Therapeutics)

Following the planning model suggests that the lesson plan should include learning activities for students. A lesson plan is not then the same as lecture notes. If an activity or type of teaching lasts too long, students lose concentration. The plan, therefore, needs to include a variety of activities.

> I'll make sure that my tutorial doesn't last longer than 30 minutes; that's the limit for students' time span for concentration. I pay attention to students' gestures. If they look as if they are about to drop off, I'll give a little recess, let them go to the restroom, or just joke with them for a bit to refresh them.
> (Francis Chan – CUHK – Medicine and Therapeutics)

Individual activity

Make a detailed plan for a class you are about to teach. Again use the three-element planning table.

Aims	Fundamental concepts	Learning activities

The class planning grid can be downloaded at
http://www.routledge.com/textbooks/9780415420259.

Flexibility

As already stated, good preparation includes making a plan for each lesson. This plan might not be stuck to precisely as the award-winning teachers were flexible in their teaching because of their interaction with students. As issues were raised by students the plan might be adapted.

> Every lesson has a predetermined structure. In other words, it needs to be prepared. But you need to be flexible within that structure when you're teaching a lesson; have the flexibility to cater for student needs or issues that you haven't thought about. It's inevitable and you'll have to deal with those when they come up. So prepare very carefully, and structure what you expect students to get out of the lesson, then be prepared to move along with that as you go on.
>
> (Allan Walker – CUHK – Educational Administration)

Teaching plans also need to be adapted so as to be in concert with the progression of students. The good teacher adapts teaching to be in harmony with current learning skills.

> Teaching is just like a dance. You need to closely look and feel your partner in the dance, if their steps are confused, if they follow the music. If you know that your partner is a bit clumsy, you will need to adjust and help your partner. Skip those difficult fancy steps until your partner reaches a certain level. There are enough lessons for you to gradually guide them and for them to catch up. They can then dance beautifully. Be patient and let them learn gradually. If they cannot dance well, I have to check on my part.
>
> (Andrew Chan – CUHK – Marketing)

To be able to flexibly adapt teaching plans, the teacher needs to continuously monitor what is going on in the classroom to obtain feedback. This feedback can come from students' comments or answers to questions. It can also be obtained by monitoring activities.

> I think it's absolutely fundamental to good teaching to be able to read the audience. The same applies whether you're dealing with a class of 130 kids or a one-to-one conversation. The first skill is to read when you've lost the audience and the second skill is to able to deal with it

when you've lost them. Now sometimes I'll get 45 minutes into a lecture and the room might be hot or it might be late in the afternoon or maybe the topic's gone a bit dry or I haven't got the energy and I'll think, 'I've lost these kids', and so I'll just say, 'Okay guys, that's enough for one day' and they'll go with relief. But you can't do that if you're only five minutes into the lecture. You have to bring them back on track with an anecdote or a shift of pace or by skipping some material to get to the crucial point. I think reading your audience is part of engaging with the students, part of treating them with dignity.

(Leonora Ritter – Charles Sturt – History, B B & P, pp. 32–33)

Some students have revealing expressions which show whether something has been understood or not, when boredom has set in and other important moods of the class. Part of getting to know your students is finding ones who are representative of the class, who have these revealing expressions.

The one I like to use is the total number of glazed looks in the audience, with my goal being zero. I know when there's been communication. You know when someone's listening to you and you know when they're not.

(Damian Conway – Monash – Computer Science, B B & P, p. 342)

Principle 8.2

Thorough planning is needed for each lesson, but plans need to be adapted flexibly in the light of feedback obtained in class.

Chapter 9

Teaching large classes

Function of lectures

In this chapter we make use of the principles derived in the earlier chapters to give some guidelines and advice for teaching large classes. The most common form of large classes in higher education is, of course, lectures.

The first point of discussion is whether lectures are consistent with some of the principles of good teaching. Principle 6.1 called for students to be actively engaged in learning activities. However, in most lectures the students are expected to be passive recipients of the lecturer's knowledge.

In Chapter 4 we established that the award-winning teachers believed that teaching was a process of facilitating student learning. Teachers who believed that teaching was a process of transmitting knowledge tended to encourage students to use a surface approach. However, the function of lectures is commonly described as transmitting knowledge.

It might seem, therefore, that good teaching is incompatible with giving lectures. However, the large majority of the award-winning teachers did give some lectures. All spent some time passing on their knowledge of their subject to their students. Even in courses which use student-centred approaches like problem-based learning, a certain body of knowledge has to be mastered. Expecting students to discover all this knowledge for themselves can be time-consuming, inefficient and tedious.

> Now we set problems, and in order to solve their problems students need to know something about Building Services. When students get to a point where they perceive the need for information, that's when they're ready to receive it and understand it. Now, instead of sitting through boring lectures once a week on dull subjects such as Building Services, students are knocking on my door saying, 'We've got to see the Services guy, right now'. I have students falling in my door demanding information on Building Services!

One of the tricks in planning a problem-based learning curriculum is trying to predict when these points will be reached. Then, instead of getting a related expert in to deliver a lecture series, we get them to come in for three hours a day on three consecutive days at the point in the process when students will be seeking their information.
(Lindsay Johnston – Newcastle – Architecture, B B & P, p. 443)

While most of the interviewees had lecture classes, none relied exclusively on lectures or taught in a way which was entirely didactic. Some indeed questioned the value of lectures.

It has been only relatively recently that I've realised that, as a vehicle for learning, the traditional lecture format is of little value. It just doesn't work very well. I realised that from my own lecturing experience; I hadn't learned very effectively from the lectures themselves. The real learning had taken place when I reflected on the material outside of the lectures, or I read about it or talked about it with colleagues.
(Michael Morgan – Monash – Physics, B B & P, p. 260)

The award-winning teachers used lecture classes in a way which was more flexible than most teachers. They were used in conjunction with other forms of teaching which were more student-centred. Lecture classes often involved student activity.

We're becoming more open to new ways of doing things. I realise I have a long way to go, but at least I'm clear that there are good reasons for changing how I teach rather than just continuing on with the same old lecturing format, because they are ineffective. I'm beginning to understand that what you've got to do in lectures is not just talk for fifty-five minutes, but that you have to try to break it up, get the students involved, do things like making them predict something and then discussing their observations.
(Michael Morgan – Monash – Physics, B B & P, p. 260)

There will be more discussion of these variations on traditional lecture formats towards the end of the chapter. First though we will draw on some of the principles to derive guidelines for teaching which involves passing on knowledge to students. For most readers this means dealing first with the familiar and then moving on to what may be less familiar, which is in itself a useful strategy.

These two references discuss when and for what purposes lectures are appropriate – or inappropriate. Both consider the qualities of a good lecture and how activities can be incorporated into lectures.

Bligh, D. A. (2000). *What's the use of lectures?* San Francisco: Jossey-Bass.
Eitington, J. E. (2002). *The winning trainer: Winning ways to involve people in learning* (4th edn) (ch. 18 'If you must lecture . . .' pp. 408–438). Boston: Butterworth-Heinemann.

Making fundamental concepts explicit

The first principle derived in Chapter 5 was that, when determining what to teach, concentrate on fundamental concepts. In this chapter we go a step further by showing how good teachers are careful to make explicit the key points. Even though the fundamental concepts may be clear to you, students often confuse the key points with the supporting materials and examples.

Simple messages are easier to understand and remember. Conveying messages in a simple and clear manner does require skills. At the start of each class, I will state very clearly the learning objectives, 'I want you to learn four things in the following half hour, they are . . .' At the end of each class, I will ask, 'What is the "take-home" message from this lesson?' Then I'll reemphasise, 'Among the four things we've learnt, if you can't remember them all, you must however not forget this very aspect as it is crucial for being a good doctor.'
(Francis Chan – CUHK – Medicine and Therapeutics)

Being able to make the fundamental concepts explicit means planning the structure of a lecture around them. Inspiring lectures sometimes seem impromptu, but there is almost certainly a well thought-out structure behind it.

I believe the deadliest sin in teaching is to read a paper or read a lecture. I never read lectures. People say I talk off the top of my head, but my lectures are actually very structured. I think there is a real skill in structuring your material, not only in being logical in yourself but also in making that logic clear to students. Over the years I've sat through other people's lectures wondering, 'Where on earth is this going?'.
(Pauline Meemeduma – James Cook – Social Work, B B & P, p. 122)

Just as the fundamental points are made explicit, the structure to
them should also be made clear by providing a road map of the les

> What I've learnt from this guy is: at the beginning of each lesson – it's so
> basic when you think about it but so many people don't do it – he told
> us what the lesson is about and what you are going to achieve. It's so
> simple when I say it but it was almost foreign to me. So right from
> the beginning of that lesson, I knew what I was doing and I knew
> what was expected.
> (Allan Walker – CUHK – Educational Administration)

Showing relevance by relating theory to practice

Principle 5.2 pointed out the need to show relevance which could be established through real-life examples, local cases, contemporary issues or relating
theory to practice. This principle is important for lectures. It is hard to
concentrate on what is being covered if you cannot see its relevance.

A way of relating theory to practice is shown in the following quotation.
Periodically students are asked to reflect upon and discuss a concept.
Relevance can be established by asking students to relate a theory to their
own experience or scenarios they are familiar with.

The example also introduces the idea of activities in lectures. It is hard to
concentrate on listening to a lecture for an hour or more. Breaking up the
exposition with periodic discussions or other activities provides rejuvena-
tion. Discussion with the person beside you, or in small groups of three or
four, works even in very large tiered lecture theatres.

> I think it's important to balance theory or research findings with prac-
> tice. Even in large lecture groups I regularly stop and encourage the
> students to reflect on what they've learned by sharing their ideas with
> a partner or in a small group. I back up the underlying principles by
> showing them a range of different strategies which I think are practical
> ways of putting those principles into practice. When we do practical
> exercises, I try to help them make the links back to the theory underly-
> ing whatever we're doing.
> (Toni Noble – ACU – Educational Psychology, B B & P, p. 222)

The next example uses a mini case study which is progressively developed.
Realistic cases show how a theory can be interpreted in practical situations.
The quotation also dwells on challenging beliefs about knowledge by showing that issues do not have a single correct answer. It is only through exposing students to messy problems that they can make the difficult transition
from seeing everything as right or wrong to making reasoned judgements
based on the evidence available.

In presenting these issues to students, I might give them a scenario, such as, 'You are coaching a star athlete. He is really slack about showing up for training and other athletes are complaining that he gets away with being late or not showing up at all. What do you do?'. They'll argue it out and then I'll add in a new fact: 'You're a paid coach and if your team loses you're going to lose your job. Does that change what you do?'. Then I might say, 'Have you considered that there might be some concerns, family problems or whatever, underlying why this athlete hasn't been showing up?'. I keep adding little bits of information and I help them to realise that there is no one right answer. This is really hard for some students, particularly those who are coming through science and are used to black-and-white answers. We're talking about theories and there just is no one right answer – but whatever answer you give, you must be able to justify it.

(Stephanie Hanrahan – Queensland – Sport Psychology, B B & P, p. 228)

Good presentations

When talking in a lecture remember the principles established in Chapter 7 about motivating students. Try to make your talk interesting. Lively anecdotes and analogies can spice up plain fare. If you have a sense of humour, use it.

What I'm hoping to achieve is for students to become interested in the subject. I don't want them to be bored, I don't want them to feel that it's irrelevant, and I don't want them to feel that it was useless being here. Beyond everything else, I want the students to feel they've got something here that they can go out and use. I guess humour is a very important way of getting the message across and building rapport with students.

(Jim McKnight – UWS – Psychology, B B & P, p. 241)

As you will see in the next chapter some, but not all, of the award-winning teachers made innovative use of computers in their teaching. Being an expert in media use is not essential to being a good teacher, but it is useful to be competent. Mastering the basics of Powerpoint is not difficult and is quite sufficient for many fine teachers.

The lecture theatre that I lecture in is one of these modern ones which has no white boards or black boards. Just a big blank wall and I in fact use my Macintosh to present materials on that. I have found the use of computer-mediated presentation to be particularly effective. Having presentation materials stored and displayed by the computer reduces the 'logistical' component of lecturing to a non-intrusive minimum – managing overhead projector slides, co-ordinating audio and video presentations, etc. Not having to shuffle overheads, switch projectors, write on a board, or manually simulate various code demonstrations, means that my attention is constantly focused on the students, which forces them to remain focused on me.

(Damian Conway – Monash – Computer Science, B B & P, p. 341)

There is such a lot of publicity about information technology nowadays that it is easy to be lured into equating proficiency in IT use with proficiency in teaching. The two are not the same though.

I surveyed the students and compared them with last year's students, and I found that the technology didn't have as big an impact as I thought it would. The students thought the presentation was nice, but it didn't really help the learning process. There's absolutely no point being innovative if it's just for the sake of innovation. It's just too much hard work. I can attest to that, having tried to utilise (or over-utilise) multimedia in my lecture presentation.

(Michael Morgan – Monash – Physics, B B & P, p. 265)

Demonstrations are possibly not used as often as they used to be. In suitable subjects a good demonstration can make a stimulating lecture class.

My favourite demonstration is the magic lantern. It's a simple little experiment. I have an incandescent touch globe connected to a radio frequency (RF) electrical power source. Now when I turn the power on the globe does not illuminate as expected. The students probably can think of many reasons to this, such as, there isn't enough power and so it doesn't glow. Then I set up a short circuit across the lamp. Now any porridge eating budding electrical engineer will be thinking, 'linear circuit theory, short circuit across the lamp, light will go out'. But it doesn't! The light comes on for reasons which are revealed by a study of the RF power! The lamp coming on and going off as the short circuit is put in place and removed is totally contrary to what they predicted. I love it!

(Bob Lord – RMIT – Communication Engineering, B B & P, p. 322)

Obtaining feedback

Chapter 14 is devoted to methods for evaluating teaching and obtaining feedback. At this point we introduce techniques which are specific to lecture classes. These can be improved if you gather feedback as you teach.

The first strategy is the simple one of maintaining eye contact with the audience. Speaking to them directly makes for a better delivery and enables you to watch the expressions. Glazed looks indicate that you have lost them, while boredom can be displayed in a variety of obvious ways.

> The understanding that teaching is communication allows me to constantly gauge my teaching performance against a quantifiable metric. The one I like to use is the total number of glazed looks in the audience, with my goal being zero. I know when there's been communication. You know when someone's listening to you and you know when they're not. There are a number of ways I can tell whether or not I'm getting through to them. The most obvious way is the noise level – as you lose them the noise level goes up. I almost never have a problem with that and when I do I hope I pick up on it very quickly. I'll break and we'll do something different or I'll say, 'What are the questions?' or 'Why are people talking?' or whatever.
> (Damian Conway – Monash – Computer Science, B B & P, p. 342)

If you have a good rapport with your students you can interact with them in a lecture class. You can simply ask them what they do not understand, why they look bored or how the class could be improved.

> I've invented the McKnight Boredom Index. I'll stop a mass lecture in the middle of a sentence and ask someone to give me an on-the-spot rating. Everyone chips in and you get surprisingly detailed feedback.
> (Jim McKnight – UWS – Psychology, B B & P, p. 241)

Reflection checklist for lectures

The following checklist can be used to reflect on lectures and large classes. It is suitable for individual reflection after a class or for use with a colleague as an observer. It can also be used in conjunction with an audio- or video-recording.

1 = needs improvement   2 = good   3 = excellent

Criteria	Rating	Comment
Introduction – clear purpose statement or roadmap		
Body – coherent logical structure		
Fundamental concepts – made explicit		
Fundamental concepts – avoided excess detail		
Relevance – gave examples to show relevance of theory		
Visual aids – helped understanding of concepts		
Delivery – spoke clearly and audibly		
Feedback – maintained eye contact for monitoring		
Conclusion – gave summary of key concepts		

Overall reflection

The reflection checklist for lectures can be downloaded at
http://www.routledge.com/textbooks/9780415420259.

Individual reflection activity

Use the reflection checklist above to reflect on your teaching in large classes. Do this for one lecture a week for a semester. Take note of aspects which could be improved and concentrate on trying to do better next time.

Activities in lectures

You must by now have realised that lecture classes by the award-winning teachers were not necessarily purely didactic, with all the talking by the lecturer. Interaction is both possible and useful once a rapport has been established with a class.

Small group discussion is possible even in tiered lecture theatres with fixed seating. Pairs form simply by turning towards the student in the next seat. Groups of four can hold a discussion if a pair turn round to talk to the pair behind them. Students who are used to sitting passively in lectures may find these activities strange at first, but soon get used to the idea.

> Many of the techniques I use to increase student-to-student talk and the time allowed for them to reflect and to personally construct their knowledge can also be used in mass lectures. If I give a mass lecture, I always try to do some paired work, some stopping and thinking, some visualising. I'll say, 'Turn to the person beside you and make a pair' or 'Make a group of four with those around you'. I think it's important to break the time up because I don't think anybody can listen for forty minutes and construct personal meaning.
> (Dawn Francis – James Cook – Education, B B & P, p. 170)

Maintaining concentration on listening throughout a lecture is not easy. Having an activity in the middle breaks up the routine. Various types of activity are possible. The following quotation describes a format for a debate. Other types of activities will be described in the next chapter. They are taken from smaller classes, but many also work in large classes.

> Another way of dealing with grey areas is to have a 'mini-debate'. I get students to pair off. Each pair is given an issue to debate, such as the use of compulsory HIV testing as a preventative technique. One student in

each pair (student A) is given a minute to argue that there should be compulsory testing. Then the other student (student B) argues that there shouldn't be, again for a minute. Student A is given thirty seconds to respond, and then they're both given a short time to summarise. Then I have a show of hands to see, within each pair, how many thought Student A won the debate, how many are convinced that B won the debate, and how many think it was a draw.

> (Stephanie Hanrahan – Queensland – Sport Psychology,
> B B & P, p. 228)

Content by other means

Those who feel that delivering lectures for students to write notes is not necessarily the most productive use of class time should realise that there are other ways of presenting knowledge. Examples are handouts which give comprehensive notes or study guides prepared for flexible or distance learning forms of a course. Materials like these can free class time for more active forms of learning.

> Since much class time is taken up by active learning sessions, we've prepared a significant amount of material in the form of a draft 'hyper-text book' which has been made available for student access via the campus computer network and the World Wide Web. This means we don't need to depend entirely on lectures to 'cover' the course content. Because this approach is still quite novel for many students, we've also taken care to induct them into the new ways of thinking required and to foster an appreciation of why we're taking these steps.
> (Chris Trevitt – ANU – Fire Science and Management, B B & P, p. 293)

If there are other means of receiving the content normally covered in lectures, some students prefer to learn from them rather than coming to lectures. Some lecturers are reluctant to give students such materials as they fear reduced attendance at lectures. An alternative interpretation is that, if students feel the materials are an acceptable substitute for a lecture, perhaps the class time (or some of it) could be used for other more fruitful learning experiences. Suggestions are: an overview of important concepts, discussion of points students find difficult, discussion of related cases or examples, and activities which give practice in applying the concepts.

> We tell our students that they don't have to attend the large groups. If they prefer, they can do self-paced learning using a study guide. The guide includes aims and objectives, introductory reading, reading required for discussion in class, reading required before the examination, and recommended reading. If the student has met the set objectives

at the end of the week, the student has learned what needed to be learned. We encourage them to come to the small groups and we give a participation grade for that.

(Marlene Le Brun – Griffith – Law, B B & P, p. 413)

Do you spend too much time lecturing?

Consider the following questions about your lectures:

1. Do you concentrate on fundamental concepts?
2. Do you show the relevance of theory with interesting examples?
3. Do you get full attendance at lectures?
4. Do your lecture classes differ significantly from the handouts or lecture notes you give your students?
5. Are your lecture notes voluminous?
6. Have you noticed students not paying attention in your lectures?
7. Do you give students a complete set of lecture notes?

If you can convincingly answer *yes* to questions 1 to 4 and *no* to questions 5 to 7, you have probably got it about right. If not, consider some of the following:

- Concentrate on key points and let students find out the rest from the handout or textbook.
- Replace some lectures with assigned readings.
- Introduce some activities.
- Divide up the topics and assign them to individuals or groups of students. Expect students to read about their topic and present it to the class.
- Expect students to have read the handout or textbook before the class. Use the class for dealing with points found to be difficult and/or practising applications.

This page can be downloaded at
http://www.routledge.com/textbooks/9780415420259.

Chapter 10

Managing discussion and group-work

Active engagement in discussion

This chapter starts by looking at the application of Principle 6.1, which calls for students to be actively engaged in learning tasks. The most common form of active learning is discussion; so that is the topic for the first part of the chapter. The rationale for discussion is that it is a form of active learning which promotes understanding.

> The reason for having so much group-work and talking is to encourage students to articulate what it is that they understand. In articulating it, they quite often discover there are some bits that they don't understand, so they have to go back and rephrase it or rethink it. In articulating it, they lay out their thinking, not only for feedback from others but also for themselves.
> (Dawn Francis – James Cook – Education, B B & P, p. 166)

The chapter also deals with group-work as many learning activities take place in small groups. The two parts of the chapter overlap considerably as discussion is the most common activity of the small groups.

Most teachers will find it easiest to implement the advice given in this chapter in smaller classes, normally designated as tutorials or seminars. As we saw in the last chapter, activities can also be incorporated into large lecture classes.

Some teachers or lecturers, who do not win awards, maintain that there is no time for discussion if they are to cover all the content they consider necessary. The retort to this is enshrined in Principle 5.1 which stresses the need to concentrate upon students reaching a thorough understanding of key concepts. If this is at the expense of covering a great body of detailed information, it is a sacrifice worth making.

> Some lecturers say, 'We have too much content, how can we fit in so much group-work?' I believe the content the students get in the end

will have more depth and be better understood as a result of the group-work. It might take a little longer to get established, but once you get going the things the students come up with are just so much richer.

(Dawn Francis – James Cook – Education, B B & P, p. 166)

What is important is how much is learnt rather than how much is covered. Students can only absorb so much. In the era of information explosion the principle of concentrating upon key concepts has become even more important.

Small groups within a class

Perhaps the greatest fear of tutors is that awful silence. They ask a question and no one responds. The way to deal with this problem is to break the students into small groups of about four to discuss the topic or question. Rather than a deadly silence the result is a lively buzz of discussion. Once the group has formulated an answer or opinion they will then be keen to tell the rest of the class; so there is no problem in getting a spokesperson to talk for the group.

In the tutorials, I break them into groups and I allow them five or ten minutes to discuss the theory questions for that week. Then they come back and one person from each group presents the group's answer.

(Christine Yap – Newcastle – Accounting, B B & P, p. 59)

The simple technique works just as well with Hong Kong students who can be rather shy and quiet in class. This is not surprising as many had little experience of discussion in school classes. Discussion in small groups deals with the inhibitions and results in a strong commitment to the consensus achieved by the group.

You have to encourage them to speak more. Give them questions ahead of time and ask them to think about it in a small group. Usually they will respond as a group. They will say, 'Our group believes this or that . . .', as they are less likely to say 'I believe this or that . . .' If you give them preparation time, usually they are pretty good about it. Normally I give them a question to think about and ask them to respond a little bit later, after the break.

(David Ahlstrom – CUHK – Management)

Discussion and activities are often managed with a pyramid structure. This starts with an individual formulating a response to a question or problem. The answer or opinion can then be discussed with another student. The pair can then combine with another pair before a spokesperson passes on the view of the quartet to the whole class. There are many variants on the pyramid structure and it provides variety if different structures are tried. Common structures are:

- individual – pair – quartet – whole class
- individual – pair – whole class
- individual – quartet – whole class.

> In think-pair-share, individual students write or simply think about their own ideas or solutions to a problem. Then they share and discuss their ideas with a partner and arrive at a consensus together. Partners may then share their ideas with another pair or with the whole class.
> (Toni Noble – ACU – Educational Psychology, B B & P, p. 219)

There are also various ways for the group to record its answer and the spokesperson to report to the whole class. The groups can record key points on chart paper or overhead transparencies to aid the spokesperson's presentation. Alternatively, the teacher can record points on a whiteboard as the summary is given. The advantage of having a written record is that it helps in giving a debriefing. Another way of passing the conclusion on is for each group to send one member to the next group to tell them their group's conclusion. This strategy works well if there are a series of activities as the groups change composition each time. A variation on this cyclical movement pattern is used in the following example.

> I frequently use jigsaw teaching. For example, recently, in a course on the Psychology of Learning, this structure was used as a means of exploring different theoretical models. The students were divided into small groups and each member in the group was given the responsibility of looking at one theoretical model. So one student was to look at the humanist model, one was to look at the behaviourist model, one was to look at the cognitive model, and so on. Their task was to develop some sound study questions on their model. For the first hour of the tutorial time, they got together with the people who had the same model from each of the other groups. So all the humanists got together, all the cognitive people got together, etc. In this hour, they developed some challenging study questions and answers on their model. Then, for the second hour, they went back to their group to teach their own group members what they considered to be the key elements of their particular model.
> (Toni Noble – ACU – Educational Psychology, B B & P, p. 219)

Group activity

This is a discussion activity we have used many times in courses for both new teachers and teaching assistants. It consistently works well and the participants become committed to their group's conclusions.

Ask the class to divide into groups of about four. Ask each group to discuss the question *What makes a good seminar or tutorial?* About 20 minutes needs to be allocated for the discussion.

Each group should summarise their conclusions on chart paper or an overhead transparency. One member of each group can then present the group's findings. If there are a lot of groups restrict each group to one point which has not been raised by another group.

At the end of the presentations the facilitator needs to debrief the activity by providing a synthesis of key points. The charts or transparencies can be collected for typing up. This way the participants can be given a record of each group's conclusion and the facilitator's synthesis.

Managing discussion

For discussion activities the teacher has the role of discussion and activity manager. The role encompasses controlling the flow of the discussion and ensuring that the activity reaches an appropriate conclusion.

> You've got to be the focal point. Even if you let the group discussion roll, you still need to be the conductor of the orchestra. Room dynamics and seating arrangements can be critical. If the person who is the most interactive in your entire tutorial is sitting at the front left hand corner, you end up having a dialogue just with them and you lose the rest. Somehow you have to get that person to go and sit at the back so the room gets brought in or you've got to redirect discussion from the front to the back and say, 'Tricia just said this, what do you think?'
>
> (Leonora Ritter – Charles Sturt – History, B B & P, p. 29)

A potentially difficult issue with managing discussion is uneven contributions. Most classes have one or two students who like to talk all the time and others who prefer to stay silent. If you break the class into subgroups you can insist on having a different spokesperson each time. That way everyone gets a turn. A graphic way of showing levels of participation is described in the following quotation.

> If I'm having trouble getting equity of participation in a group, I use a ball of wool. I put the students into a circle of ten. As each person

speaks, they take the ball of wool and then hold onto the twine as they pass the ball onto the next person who speaks. After five or ten minutes we stop and look at the design appearing in the wool.

(Dawn Francis – James Cook – Education, B B & P, p. 165)

There are times when the uneven participation is because of the teacher talking too much. It is easy for this to happen because the teacher has the expertise in the topic. However, monologues do not make effective discussion classes. Students can be brought into the discussion through questions.

My perception is teachers generally talk too much. You can tell somebody's puzzled by the way they look. And you can tell if somebody is not paying attention, often because I'm talking too much. You can tell that somebody is subtly drifting off; that's the time to ask questions, to get them moving and to keep them in. It's monitoring what's going on really. I try and make it so that I don't talk more than 50–60% of the time at most. The rest of the time is students'. Whenever I teach, I have all these questions I'm going to ask them about.

(Gordon Mathews – CUHK – Anthropology)

Asking questions

The most common way of managing discussion in tutorials and seminars is asking questions. Participation can be managed by selecting students to answer questions, though this has to be done carefully to avoid embarrassing the shyer students or those who have no ready response to a particular question.

Usually, the more enthusiastic ones answer the questions, so I try to bring in the quieter ones. If they don't answer, I just move on to someone else. I don't try to embarrass them at all. I encourage them to come forward, and to not feel inhibited by being in the class.

(Derek Henry   RMIT – Nursing, B B & P, p. 364)

The initial question needs to be an open one if a meaningful discussion is to happen. If there is hesitancy in responding it can be because students are not sure where to start with the open question. In this case try some prompting questions to channel the direction of the discussion and to explore the topic. These prompting questions are essentially breaking down the big open question into subquestions which are easier to answer. Probing questions can then be used to lead the discussion towards deeper and more insightful conclusions from an initial response. Common probing questions are variations on *how?* and *why?*

I use a lot of questioning techniques to see if they've understood. So when a group is doing an introductory five minutes at the beginning of class I question them: 'Are you sure that's going to be appropriate at that time, and why do you want to use it?'

(Christine Hogan – Curtin – Management, B B & P, p. 70)

Questions can also be used as responses to student questions. Providing an answer when you are asked a question often does not help the students to learn how to solve problems themselves. Breaking a larger open problem down into a series of more straightforward questions can help students start doing this themselves.

I like to give students problem sheets where I tease out some of the little problems they're likely to encounter with particular concepts. If the students just apply the formulae by rote, they'll trip up. That's a deliberate ploy that I use to make them go back and think again. When they ask me a question, I try to identify the gap in their understanding and then pose a series of simpler questions designed to lead them from their current understanding to a new deeper understanding. This new deeper understanding will enable the student to answer the original question for themselves.

(Bob Lord – RMIT – Communication Engineering, B B & P, p. 321)

Activity in pairs

Practice questioning techniques in pairs. Pick an open topic which both of you are familiar with. Take it in turn to play the role of teacher and student. The teacher should go through a series of open, prompting and probing questions to draw out a good response.

Discussion activities

If discussion sessions are to work well there needs to be a good activity or discussion topic. One source of activities is published papers.

In seminars, we will discuss some newly published papers and analyse the strength and the weaknesses or limitations of the study, and whether the conclusion is credible. Most importantly, I'll ask them, 'If you come across a similar case, will you adopt the new treatment or will you prefer the old? Is the new treatment method supported by adequate evidence? Or would you rather wait and see?' This is to train them to think.

(Gregory Cheng – CUHK – Medicine and Therapeutics)

A good guide to designing activities is Principle 5.2. If students can see the relevance of a discussion topic or activity they are likely to engage in it seriously. Relevance can be established through current issues, local examples or practical real-life cases.

> In one of the courses I teach, I try to conduct discussion sessions once every two weeks. Students are organized into groups of three to five. Before the discussion, I give them some open-ended problems to solve rather than regular homework. These are problems without definite answers which students may need to research beforehand on the web. They are supposed to do it independently.
>
> Come the date of discussion, students will gather together and discuss among themselves. TAs and I will walk around to answer questions, anything that is unclear in their mind. But we will not give out answers. There are no definite answers. One week later, they have to submit a report. . . . In general, they like it.
>
> Q: What kind of problems do you give out in these discussion sessions? Practical problems. If a certain company is producing one kind of product, I will ask them to check what kind of product it is. How does it relate to what they have learnt in terms of technical implementation? How do they think the engineers in this company implement this product? What are the advantages and disadvantages? This would arouse their thinking better than just learning a programming language and doing a programming assignment.
>
> (Soung Liew – CUHK – Information Engineering)

Discussion activities are an important way of implementing Principle 5.3 which notes that there may be a need to challenge students' existing beliefs. Confronting them with unexpected outcomes is a way to do this.

> I often use the system of Predict, Observe, Explain as the learning method. I explain this method to the learners and get them to look at something, find it's different from what they expect it to be, and have them nut out why they made the wrong prediction. When they find they can use this learning to correctly deal with new but different situation, then they aren't just rote learning. I think learning is when you change your behaviour or you change your understanding. It's when you attempt a problem and you check your answer and find it's incorrect that you see you have a chance to learn and that to do this you must change your behaviour. That's what I think learning is. And that sort of learning can go on forever – the great thinkers of the world, people like Einstein, keep trying to understand what makes the world tick and end up searching for the meaning of life.
>
> (Bob Lord – RMIT – Communication Engineering, B B & P, p. 321)

Individual or group activity

Plan one activity which you can use in a class you teach which students will find really interesting. Interesting activities are likely to show how a theory relates to current or local issues.

Debriefing

At the conclusion of discussion activities it is important to have a debriefing to ensure that students take the key concepts from the lesson. Without a debriefing some will instead remember discussion points they found interesting, but which are not central. A good teacher should draw out from the discussion the key conclusions.

> After the interviews, the tutorial leaders conduct debriefing sessions in which they summarise the information gained and recommend further reading.
> (Justine Alison – James Cook – Nursing, B B & P, p. 358)

Students can also be asked to contribute to the debriefing. The advantage of involving students is that they learn that a set of set of key points is an appropriate outcome for a learning exercise. It does sometimes need a degree of control from the teacher to ensure that the appropriate conclusion is drawn.

> I always assign equal time to participating in an activity and reflecting on the learning from that activity. Towards the end of the session, I go back to the objectives to see how well we've met them. . . . Then we move around the circle in turn with everybody giving feedback about something interesting they've learned or something they've had difficulty with.
> (Dawn Francis – James Cook – Education, B B & P, p. 165)

A somewhat different type of debriefing is needed when students go to different practice situations. At the end of the practice period it is valuable to bring them together to discover what each has learnt and for them to learn from each others' experiences.

> As a result of students' comments in their journals, I introduced debriefing sessions. Generally, I get six or seven students together for a one-hour debriefing session. This gives them the opportunity to hear about what the others are doing.
> (Elaine Thompson – UNSW – Political Science, B B & P, p. 93)

Reflection checklist

The following checklist can be used to reflect on seminars and tutorials. It is suitable for individual reflection after a class or for use with a colleague as an observer. It can also be used in conjunction with an audio- or video-recording.

1 = needs improvement   2 = good   3 = excellent

Criteria	Rating	Comment
Planning – planned content and activities		
Time management – planning and execution		
Organisation – prepared teaching materials		
Introduction – purpose established at start		
Activities – clear direction and management		
Questioning – managed discussion with questions		
Questioning – used range of prompts and probes		
Flexibility – adapted plans in response to feedback		
Debriefing – summarised key concepts		

 The reflection checklist for seminars and tutorials can be downloaded at http://www.routledge.com/textbooks/9780415420259.

Individual reflection on small group teaching

Use the reflection checklist to reflect upon your own teaching in seminars and tutorials. Do this over a semester and try to make iterative improvements.

Group-work

This section on group-work relates to what has come before in this chapter in that, for much of the discussion activities, students have been formed into small within-class groups for the discussions. There is also a relationship with the next chapter, which deals with a wide variety of forms of teaching and learning, all of which promote active student engagement, rather than passive learning from didactic teaching. Many of these types of teaching can involve students working together in groups.

Why group-work?

There are several arguments for group activities. The first is that the negotiation, discussion and exploration of ideas within groups encourage the use of higher-order intellectual capabilities. This leads to the development of critical and creative thinking abilities. Interpersonal and communication skills are also practised and this leads to an improvement in them.

> Co-operative learning has a number of very positive student outcomes. Students are being active learners rather than passive recipients. They're communicating with each other about their ideas. They're making eye contact rather than sitting in rows and just looking out at the front. They're taking responsibility for coming up with their own ideas rather than just being given ideas by me. They are more motivated to stay on task and spend longer working on a problem or an issue than they would be as an individual.
>
> Co-operative learning strategies give students the opportunity to hear and respect other points of view. This is critical in encouraging reflection on their own beliefs and attitudes. Students have to think about where they stand on an issue, clarify their point of view to others and evaluate differing views. So I think it encourages higher order thinking and leads to deeper learning rather than just surface learning. Students are given the opportunity to practice and learn interpersonal, communication and teamwork skills.
>
> (Toni Noble – ACU – Educational Psychology, B B & P, p. 220)

A lot of learning takes place in groups – often a lot more than when students sit passively listening to a teacher.

> I think that students teach each other much more than we teach them. Perhaps it's a good quality for a teacher to allow this peer learning to take place, but sometimes it can get a little frightening.
>
> (Justine Alison – James Cook – Nursing, B B & P, p. 361)

Group, rather than individual, projects or activities also permit students to tackle more substantial tasks. This means that they can be asked to deal with more complex real-life issues rather than simplified tasks.

> I think the students actually learn a lot more if they're forced to interact with each other in a group and they get to bounce ideas off each other. Of course, there's the added advantage that they can get things done more quickly because there are three or four people to do things instead of just one.
>
> (Alan Butler – Adelaide – Zoology, B B & P, p. 284)

Arranging groups

When forming groups, opinion is divided between allowing students to choose their own group-mates and selecting groups for them. One award-winning teacher made a very graphic case for allowing students to form their own groups.

> In group assessment, I allow students a fair amount of flexibility in how they compose their groups. The literature suggests you should find out students' assets and liabilities and then allocate them to groups so that their skills are spread evenly and they'll all learn from each other. I tried to do that once, but it didn't work. We have huge numbers of part-time students from a great variety of backgrounds. I could have one student who is a business person downtown, has very little time, is earning ninety thousand dollars and driving a BMW who really doesn't want to talk to this full-time student who's got pimples, is living in Kogarah or Hurstville or Penrith, and who wants to meet out there. And in this group you've also got the housewife who comes from Wollongong who's trying to manage a family and arrange babysitting, which can be difficult. And I'm telling these people to get together to do a group project! That's why it failed. . . . I now let students choose their own groups.
>
> (Mark Freeman – UTS – Economics and Finance, B B & P, p. 46)

Another argued for teachers to allocate students to groups.

> Given that students put so much energy into the subgroups, I try to
> ensure that nobody gets stuck in a dysfunctional group. One way of
> doing this is for staff to allocate students to subgroups. I have found
> that if I let them choose their own subgroups, the result will be two
> pretty functional groups of, say, six or seven each, and the third group
> will have students who do not readily identify with other people in the
> room and who almost certainly do not readily identify with each other,
> and that group is much more likely to be dysfunctional. It is not
> possible to completely avoid the occasional dysfunctional group, but
> the impact of this is ameliorated by changing the group membership
> mid-semester, so that no one should be in a dysfunctional subgroup
> for the whole semester.
>
>   (Peter Lee – South Australia – Social Work, B B & P, p. 111)

We allow students to form their own groups – partly because that is
normally their preference and partly because you rarely have sufficient information about individuals' interpersonal and group-work skills to make a
good job of forming compatible and productive groups.

Group dsyfunctionality can be reduced by checking progress on a regular
basis and discussing task management with those who do not appear to be
progressing well. A further strategy for improving group performance and
making assessment fairer is to use one of the methods for group members
to assess each other's contribution to the work of the group. These ask
each student to rate the contribution of each other group member to specified aspects of the project work. Marks for the group can then be adjusted
according to contributions. This rewards those who have put in the most
effort and penalises the freeloaders. Assessment of contribution to group
projects is discussed in more detail towards the end of Chapter 12.
References are given to articles which give detailed descriptions of how to
organise and conduct the peer assessment.

Facilitation

Facilitating group-work is a delicate balancing act. Intruding too much
within a group removes the benefits which accrue from the self-directing
nature of group activities. On the other hand, having no contact with
groups can mean that some groups go off in directions which are unproductive and dysfunctional groups can flounder. A reasonable middle point is to
arrange review meetings at regular intervals with each group. Progress and
direction are then checked periodically.

The other point of balance which is important is the degree of direction
given to a group. Excessive prescription turns a project into an exercise in

following a recipe. An absence of directions can lead to blind alleyways or going round and round in circles. A useful technique is to use probing questions to prompt students to work out a direction for themselves. A good example is in the quotation below.

> Here's an example of how a demonstrator might provide guidance. You might say to students that you want them to investigate a particular species of snail, where it is on the shore, why it's there and not somewhere else. So they might go into a huddle and say, 'Right, we've got to do a transect here – we'll need a tape measure and string and levelling devices and quadrants and so on'. The demonstrator will say, 'Okay, but why? Why do you want to do a transect?' It turns out they want to do a transect because they learned how to do a transect in another course, and they'll be a bit stunned by someone asking them why they want to do it. Their initial response will be pretty much 'Because we've already learned that this is the right thing to do'. So the demonstrator is essentially saying, 'Well, it may be or it may not be the right thing to do; it's your responsibility to decide why you're doing it'. This usually stuns them.
>
> (Alan Butler – Adelaide – Zoology, B B & P, p. 283)

Computer conferencing

Most group discussion takes place face-to-face. It is also possible for it to be computer-based. For distance education students this provides a vital channel for interaction which they would otherwise be denied. Computer-based communication can also be used as a supplement to face-to-face classes. Groups of students can continue their dialogue outside the classroom.

> I've come up with an idea I've called 'computer-supported collaborative problem-based learning'. Problem-based learning is about focusing the learning and instructional process within the context of a problem – making it more authentic, more realistic for the learner. I asked myself how we could bring the technology, collaborative learning principles and problem-based learning together in a composite environment. So I've developed a model that can also be applied in a face-to-face classroom. You present the problem during the lecture, then you embark on a process of investigating, negotiating and exploring the problem in a computer-supported environment.
>
> We create virtual tutorial groups on what we call the 'Listserv', to which students have access through the university computer labs. Firstly, they post their individual reflections on a problem to the tutorial group. When they've all placed their reflections, they can read each other's

reflections, just as they would in a face-to-face tutorial. At the next stage, they go away and revise their initial reflection and think about whether their view of the issue may have changed after considering the others' responses. They can then return and bring in, for example, articles that may be relevant to the problem. Finally, they produce a 'critical reflection record' summing up everything that's transpired in relation to the problem.

The objective is to get people to discuss the issues and reflect on the problem from a variety of viewpoints. We're simply creating an environment for people to have a discussion if they want to. As the lecturer, I might come in every now and then and pick up on things, make a comment from my own experiences and give general feedback. I don't necessarily read all the comments in great detail every day so monitoring the whole process is not too much of a task. I allocate half an hour every second day to it. We spend that kind of time on our electronic mail every day anyway.

(Som Naidu – Southern Queensland – Education, B B & P, p. 186)

Chapter 11

Ways of encouraging active learning

Variety of approaches

The previous two chapters have discussed the most common types of university teaching: lectures, seminars and tutorials. All of the CUHK award-winning teachers used other additional forms of teaching and learning. Many of the stories of the Australian award-winning teachers concentrated on an innovative form of teaching. Quality in teaching should not be equated to innovation, but variety was definitely a feature of the award-winners' teaching.

> Good teaching involves things like projects, self-directed laboratory work, individual tasks, informal small group sessions, participation through tutorials – with students not just sitting at the desk, but actually coming out to the board. Sometimes the most effective learning takes place when the students come to speak to you about an unrelated issue and then, as you get talking, they say, 'Oh by the way, I want to know about this'. Good teaching can mean a whole range of things. I don't think you can do it using any one vehicle. I think you're more likely to capture the essence of good teaching with diversity.
> (Michael Morgan – Monash – Physics, B B & P, p. 267)

The following quotation shows how a concept can be developed through a variety of teaching approaches. Each relates to the theme in a contrasting way, and so communication is explored from different perspectives. Yet each is designed to contribute to the overall goal of encouraging self reflection.

> I think there should be a main theme. For example, if I am teaching communication, there should be verbal and nonverbal communication. Students may observe the above areas in non-classroom settings. Eye contact and verbal communication are means of communication.
> I tried to let students have a feel about communication. I request some help from students who are fluent orally. I asked a student to

explain verbally a selected object, such as a bottle. I then asked other students as an audience to draw a picture about the object. The students spent about five minutes. I allowed the audience to ask questions. After the question and answer session, some audience members started to modify the picture that they had drawn. I let students express their feelings about the whole process. This is a good exercise in a way that students can play opposite roles and respect each role's perspective.

I also share teaching experiences with students and demonstrate to them the ways I handle each situation. Sometimes, I ask students to fill in a questionnaire to know more about their psychological state. Videos are used to assist the lecture and enrich the discussion.

All of the above activities are designed to encourage self reflection. I think self reflection is crucial in a teacher training programme. A teacher with good reflection skills would review his techniques and knowledge.

(Patrick Lau – CUHK – Educational Psychology)

This chapter is, therefore, devoted to expounding on a combination of Principle 6.1, which calls for students to be actively engaged in a variety of learning tasks, and the last part of Principle 7.1, which notes that students can be motivated by a variety of active learning approaches. The remainder of the chapter gives an outline of the more commonly used methods. In each case references are given so that those who decide to adopt a particular approach will be able to learn enough about it to do so.

Projects

Projects are a student-centred form of learning. The students acquire knowledge for themselves rather than from the teacher, though the teacher does have a role to play as a guide and facilitator. Projects take on a variety of forms, depending particularly on the discipline, but all involve student participation in a role consistent with that of practitioners in the field.

Projects are a type of learning in their own right, but are also constituents of some of the other types of teaching which follow. Problem-based learning and role-plays, for example, have projects of a particular form as an integral component.

We deliberately chose to work with first year students. Some of my colleagues predicted this would not succeed because they have the idea students have to have a lot of knowledge before they can do something with that knowledge. My view, however, is that students learn at the time when they need to know. This 'just-in-time' process means that as they do the research and perform the task, they call on their discipline knowledge and apply this discipline knowledge in context. In the process, they also learn to value the kinds of strengths that people from other disciplines bring with them.

One project commissioned by the Ballarat Gold Fields involved putting geological information into hypertext for Years 11 and 12 students. Both geology and computing students volunteered to work on this project. At the beginning, the geology students didn't have all the knowledge that was needed to develop the maps, and the computing students didn't know how to get the maps into hypertext. So they each went and got support from their lecturers in their own disciplines. So what we're actually doing is creating a situation in which students are seeking knowledge rather than just being given it.

(Wendy Crebbin – Ballarat – Education, B B & P, p. 142)

An interesting point about this quotation is that the projects were for first year students. It is probably more common for projects to occur later in degrees, and they are often treated as the culmination of a degree programme. By this stage students know just about everything they are going to learn from their degree; so the project is their chance to put it into practice. However, they may have lost interest in the discipline by then after course learning basic knowledge. They could also benefit from early exposure to the experience of realistic work in the discipline or profession, as many students select a field with little idea of what it entails.

Action research

Action research is a project which follows the action research method and paradigm.

Students work through the Action Research Planner by Kemmis and McTaggart. They have to identify a problem in their workplace that they want to do something about, preferably with a group of people rather than on their own. We suggest they draw up a 'Table of Intervention' which includes all the factors in the situation, all the things impinging on them such as, for instance, a new syllabus, the school principal, the students, other teachers, their own time. This becomes a very nice little matrix. If certain things come up again and again, these are probably the things that are problematic for the student, things they can actually work on. People can come up with pretty good problems that they need to solve. Students choose an issue or an area of interest and then they put together an action group. They have to describe who will be involved, how they will set up the group and what their first action step will be. They then submit this plan as their first assignment.

The difficulty most beginners face with action research – and I've been one so I know what it's like – is narrowing the thematic concern to something that's small enough to actually achieve. For example, a student might say, 'My problem is that nobody on my staff uses the CSF. I'm the principal and I've got to "make" them'. Indeed that might be a problem, but it's far too big to be addressed by any one piece of research. So the students need this sort of feedback when designing their research project.

(Jo-Anne Reid – Deakin – Education, B B & P, p. 201)

Kember, D. and Kelly, M. (1993). *Improving teaching through action research*. Green Guide 14. Cambelltown, NSW: Higher Education Research and Development Society of Australasia.
Kemmis, S. and McTaggart, R. (eds) (1988). *The action research planner* (3rd edn). Geelong, Victoria: Deakin University Press.

Student presentations

Student presentations can be a type of learning method in their own right. Certain topics in the curriculum are allocated to individual students or to groups. The students are then responsible for researching the topic and teaching it to the class. Used in this way the student presentations are a form of peer teaching.

They have presentations to do as well. You'll give them a topic and they have to prepare to present and then lead discussions afterwards. Most students like that given they have the time. This is done when they have been given some foundation knowledge. We'll encourage them to look up the most advanced information on the internet.

(Gregory Cheng – CUHK – Medicine and Therapeutics)

Presentations can also be an integral part of other forms of teaching and learning. Projects, case-based teaching, problem-based learning, experiential learning and other types as well can include a presentation in which what has been learnt is reported to the rest of the class.

Student presentations can be a motivating form of assessment. Business students are normally very conservative, but they come up with some fabulous work and do all sorts of innovative things. They'll get dressed up and go onto the ferry and interview people. They'll present everything from parliamentary debates to judgements. I show videos to the students of what past students have done and every year the standard

improves. What I'm trying to get across to students is that learning is more than just absorbing a few facts.
(Mark Freeman – UTS – Economics and Finance, B B & P, p. 45)

Case-based teaching

Case-based teaching and problem-based learning share a common starting point. The starting point is an open case or problem which is usually based on a real-life scenario. This means that the problem does not have a single well-defined answer and often there are multiple issues or problems which need to be identified.

> The basic principle underlying problem-based learning is that the start-ing point for learning should be a problem that the learner wishes to solve. Courses are constructed and taught using problems as the stimu-lus and principal focus of student activity. These problems or situations are based on professional practice, rather than on formal input from experts. Problem-based learning is particularly appropriate for voca-tionally oriented courses since it avoids the theory/ practice dichotomy, the two being integrated from the beginning.
> (Peter Lee – South Australia – Social Work, B B & P, p. 104)

Case-based teaching and problem-based learning can be seen as the poles of a spectrum for teaching and learning using cases or ill-defined problems. Case-based teaching often takes up a small part of an otherwise convention-ally taught course. Pure problem-based learning can take over the curricu-lum for an entire programme. All learning focuses around the problems. Students are expected to determine what knowledge they need to deal with the problems and search for it themselves. The following quotations in this section illustrate a move across the spectrum from within-class uses of cases to a major open-ended problem.

> I will always start a course with a case and add variations as I go along so as to induce student thinking from different angles. For instance, a case of stomach bleeding, 'If a patient vomits blood in front of you, what will you do?' When an answer is given, I will then progress, 'If he has vomited so much that he faints, and your senior is unavailable, what will you do?'
> (Francis Chan – CUHK – Medicine and Therapeutics)

The example below is at a similar point of the spectrum. Notice that again the case is used within a class and the teacher elaborates the case as the lesson progresses. This quotation illustrates the use of cases for dealing with

Principle 5.3. Naïve epistemological beliefs can be challenged by exposure to messy problems without well-defined answers.

> In presenting these issues to students, I might give them a scenario, such as, 'You are coaching a star athlete. He is really slack about showing up for training and other athletes are complaining that he gets away with being late or not showing up at all. What do you do?'. They'll argue it out and then I'll add in a new fact: 'You're a paid coach and if your team loses you're going to lose your job. Does that change what you do?'. Then I might say, 'Have you considered that there might be some concerns, family problems or whatever, underlying why this athlete hasn't been showing up?'. I keep adding little bits of information and I help them to realise that there is no one right answer. This is really hard for some students, particularly those who are coming through science and are used to black-and-white answers. We're talking about theories and there just is no one right answer – but whatever answer you give, you must be able to justify it.
>
> (Stephanie Hanrahan – Queensland – Sport Psychology,
> B B & P, p. 228)

The following example is a more complex case. Like most ill-defined problems which professionals have to deal with it is multidisciplinary. The real-life relevance was very clear as the problem dealt with an issue which was central to students enrolled in the course.

> For example, in one session in environmental psychology we were analysing housing practices and looking at sustainable building. I had two young couples in my class who had met and married while in university. We sat down and analysed the standard path of a young couple saving up for a mortgage and buying a home. We used these two couples as a case-in-point. We looked at how they could go about getting a mortgage in the traditional way and then we explored other ways in which they could house themselves. The discussion included analysing housing patterns, taxation law, self-build co-operatives, etc. This allowed the students to not only see the theoretical component but also to bring it back to real life. The two couples actually followed the script that we worked out in class and ended up owning their own homes within five years.
>
> (Jim McKnight – UWS – Psychology, B B & P, pp. 236–237)

📖   Kolodner, J. L., Owensby, J. N. and Guzdial, M. (2004). Case-based learning aids. In D. H. Jonassen (ed.), *Handbook of research for education communications and technology* (2nd edn) (pp. 829–861). Mahwah, NJ: Lawrence Erlbaum Associates.

Problem-based learning

The next quotation is close to the problem-based learning end of the spectrum. The problem is a realistic architectural design project. The multi-disciplinary nature of the project is again apparent.

Students undertake a further half-semester program designing a high-rise project in a city CBD. We use a real-life problem as the trigger, something along the lines of the following scenario: 'There is a major central city site for sale in Sydney. A developer walks into an architect's office and requests the architect to prepare a concept design for the site, to establish what floor area of development can be achieved, to do technical reports on structure, construction, services, environmental issues, and so on.' The student is required to respond to this request with a comprehensive design proposal and to supply additional information including an architect's fee proposal, a business plan for the professional services associated with the project, and a bid for the site based on an assessment of the cost of development and the financial return from the development.
(Lindsay Johnston – Newcastle – Architecture, B B & P, pp. 440–441)

Tutoring problem-based learning

Tutoring problem-based learning courses calls for the facilitation skills described in the previous chapter. Direction which is over-prescriptive takes away the advantages of the problem-based approach. Lack of guidance can result in important issues being missed or inefficient use of time as unproductive avenues are followed. Again good questioning techniques provide a way to find a point of balance.

If they miss an obvious issue, I will ask questions to try to direct them toward it, but I certainly will never say, 'Look, you have missed this out'. The purpose is essentially for them to define what they see as the central themes. There will of course be times when they might miss some of the issues the problem has been designed to address. For example, in the juvenile justice scenario mentioned above, the issue of confidentiality may be missed because they will be focusing on the young people and the law and not thinking about themselves as the worker. If this happens, I might say something like, 'Well, you've dealt with lots of issues in relation to John and Paul. Are there issues for other people in this scenario, do you think?'. Hopefully this will lead them to examine the issues for the other main actors in the scenario, including the worker. However I have not signalled in any way that they should look at confidentiality – they need to come to this themselves – but I have signalled that they may need to look at the situation a bit more broadly.

I also give a strong message that there is no one right answer to any of the problems they deal with in the tutorial. When using this methodology the tutor ensures that the major issues are looked at, but there are also a whole range of peripheral issues. This means that each sub-group will have a different response to the problem. They will each deal with some common core issues but, depending on the interests of the people in the group, they will also follow a range of tangents and often come up with some really interesting material.

(Peter Lee – South Australia – Social Work, B B & P, p. 105)

1. *University of Adelaide's Centre for Learning and Professional Development (CLPD)* hosts the 'Leap' website. This is a very informative site and is a good staring point for those who are new to problem-based learning and other innovative teaching strategies. Retrieved February 20, 2006, from http://www.adelaide.edu.au/clpd/materia/leap/

2. *University of Delaware site on problem-based learning* Retrieved February 20, 2006, from http://www.udel.edu/pbl/

University of Delaware PBL Clearinghouse (you have to register but it is free) Retrieved February 20, 2006, from https://chico.nss.udel.edu/Pbl/

Role-play

A role-play normally involves a case. As the name suggests, in a role-play the students act out the parts in the case.

A role-play is set in a fictional Latin American republic that is experiencing various capitalist crises or going through a socialist revolution. About five or six weeks in advance of the role-play, I distribute a description of the situation and the roles. On a separate sheet is the agenda of topics to be covered at the meeting. The students then choose a role: an army officer, landowner, banker, peasant, or student leader. These roles represent significant social, economic and political interests of the place and time with which the situation is concerned. The students then research the role they're to play and the positions they should take on the agenda issues. As a guide to the students, I also provide a syllabus of readings which refer to some of the major issues informing the situations that are to be played out. These issues, and the accompanying readings, are discussed in our class meetings prior to the role-play. By the time we begin the role-play – normally about six or seven weeks into the session – the students should be fully prepared. Concurrently, they're preparing an essay which reflects the position they plan to take in the discussion.

As an example, let's assume our student is 'the general'. He or she must take a position on military matters, of course, but the military person is also going to have to confront issues like agrarian reform or patterns of industrialisation or even the military's relationship with the church. So I ask the person who takes on the role of the general to not merely focus on the problem of the military but to also consider the military's place in relationship to other institutions in society. It is helpful for students to watch how others are playing out their roles and how they're responding. This gives them a much broader picture of the problem. For this reason, each student has a responsibility to prepare properly. The general can only learn about the church's position or the labourer's position when the labourer or the cleric is properly prepared and able to contribute.

One advantage of using fictitious countries is that the students can't say there is only one solution. They have to look at the examples of Cuba, Nicaragua and Chile, generalise from those three situations and apply their understanding to a totally fictitious situation. They're not allowed to concoct their own solutions.

(James Levy – UNSW – History, B B & P, pp. 14–15)

Eitington, J. E. (2002). *The winning trainer: Winning ways to involve people in learning* (4th edn) (pp. 105–138). Boston: Butterworth-Heinemann.

Reflective journals

Reflective journals aim to encourage students to reflect upon their learning by recording their reflections in writing. This learning activity has probably been more commonly applied in professional programmes. A rationale was provided by Schön (1983) who observed that the ability to perform a professional role depended more on the ability to think reflectively in the context of professional practice, than on accumulated knowledge.

> A lot of students feel a bit threatened by the reflective journal when they first start off, so I build a lot of structure into it until they develop their confidence. There are four parts to it: (1) a brief summary (I stress 'brief') of the workshops they've been engaged in; (2) any new ideas or new learning that came out of that workshop for them; (3) any questions, issues, or mismatches between what we're doing and what they're doing in other subjects; and (4) how they feel about the particular activities, group-work and so on. They start off with that sort of structure but I encourage them to develop their own style of journaling because I want the journal to be their own.
>
> (Dawn Francis – James Cook – Education, B B & P, p. 168)

Their use, though, is certainly not confined to professional subjects. They can also be used in subjects like theoretical physics as a way of revealing understanding of fundamental concepts.

> Students also have a log book in which they record what they're doing and why they're doing it. They give examples of the techniques they've learned and used. We give them a grade for this, but I also use their log book entries to sit down with them in the laboratory and say, 'Well look, last week you handed this in and you've really missed the point here; I thought you really understood this but you don't, so let's go back and have another look at it'.
>
> (Michael Morgan – Monash – Physics, B B & P, p. 265)

An interesting example combines reflective writing with more graphic reflections.

> The students are required to look around Melbourne and discover five structures they find interesting. They then present these as case studies in their diary, which they keep through the semester. They have to classify the structures and draw diagrams of them using structural notation. They have to write a short piece about how they feel about each structure, their personal response to the spatial environment created by the structure, and they have to link it to an historical example.
>
> (Robyn Lines – RMIT – Architecture, B B & P, p. 449)

Bain, J. D., Ballantyne, R., Mills, C. and Lester, N. C. (2002). *Reflecting on practice: Student teachers' perspectives.* Flaxton, Qld: Post Pressed.

Kember, D. et al. (2001). *Reflective teaching and learning in the health professions.* Oxford: Blackwell Science.

Schön, D. A. (1983). *The reflective practitioner: How professionals think in action.* New York: Basic Books.

Experiential learning

Experiential learning involves students in learning by performing a role related to their discipline or professional area. Many professional pro-grammes include periods spent practising the intended profession. There are many issues involved in designing a curriculum in which the professional practice gels with time in the university. Arranging and supervising the time spent in the practice situation can also be problematic.

> We've developed a fieldwork model in which field placements are closely integrated with academic content. Students undertake learning units in areas of OT practice, Paediatrics for example. Each learning unit consists of a PBL case scenario in the area of practice, together with lab sessions on specific skills relevant to the case scenario. This is then followed by a short placement in Paediatrics so that students can apply their learning. This means that when students undertake field-work they are already oriented in the area of practice, they are able to participate more fully and sooner, and they are able to transfer their learning more readily from one setting to another.
>
> Rather than having one placement of seven or eight weeks each year, our students now get three or four shorter placements each year. This enables us to integrate the placement areas with the learning units, and it has the added advantages that if the placement isn't working out the students aren't stuck there for too long. Because each student has three or four supervisors each year, we are able to develop a good overview of where the student is at. Students are able to compare and contrast different approaches and so develop their own personal ethic in relation to their practice.
>
> (Lynette Mackenzie – Newcastle – Occupational Therapy,
> B B & P, p. 394)

An internship is similar to a period of professional practice. In this case the student is fulfilling an associated role.

In the intern program, a student is attached as a research intern for one or two days a week to a politician usually, but also to organisations such as the Commonwealth Bank, the Australian Law Reform Commission or the Human Rights Commission. During their time as an intern, students may be involved in undertaking projects, writing speeches, researching for background briefings, or reporting on committees for the politician.

(Elaine Thompson – UNSW – Political Science, B B & P, p. 89)

In the following example the experiential learning takes place in class. The students learn about organisations and management by applying concepts to the organisation of a large class.

Class-as-organisation is not a role-play or simulation. It is studying the class's own behaviour and processes and dealing with problems and issues of organisational life in the classroom. These issues clearly have direct parallels with the experiences of organisations out there in the 'real world' and include: How does work get allocated? How does one motivate uncommitted or bored members? How does one work with others in small and large teams? What rules are needed concerning absenteeism or 'freeloading' in group-work? How can disagreements be resolved? How should decisions be made?

We deal with large class sizes by dividing the students into autonomous Divisions of eighty, each under the direction of two staff members who act as Divisional Managers. Each Division is further subdivided into Work Groups of twenty. Each Work Group is managed by two student Work Group Managers, thus creating a layer of 'middle management'. These are elected by and from the student members in each of the Work Groups. This structure enables us to provide experiential learning to a group of over 300 students! It's the only course I know of where this is being done with such a large group.

(Trevor Tyson – Swinburne – Management and Organisations,
B B & P, pp. 76–77)

The classic text by David Kolb is still a good starting point.

Kolb, D. A. (1984). *Experiential learning: Experience as the source of learning and development*. Englewood Cliffs, NJ: Prentice Hall.

Peer tutoring

Peer tutoring means that fellow students act as tutors to other students. Normally the peer tutors are from a higher year than the students they are tutoring. The peer tutors often learn as much, if not more, than their tutees. They can make very good tutors too.

> Third year Human Resource Management students who've been through the subject are available to the group for consultation and mentoring. We call them 'mentors' but they are more like peers. They come in and say, 'Look, I know how you feel – they did it to us too and we got through it and we did this and we did that'. It makes a huge difference. We're very reliant on the student mentors and they become like assistant managers, basically. They help a great deal at the beginning, especially with their anecdotes about how they felt. They have endless stories to tell, and I think the students believe the mentors much more than they believe us.
> (Trevor Tyson – Swinburne – Management and Organisations,
> B B & P, p. 78)

For peer tutoring to work successfully there needs to be some form of reward for the tutors. One way to do this is to make the tutoring an assessed component of a course. This can be justified as the tutoring role can help in developing the types of generic competencies discussed in Chapter 4. Some projects have paid tutors, but there is a danger of them ceasing to operate when the project funds run out.

> In the second year, I invited the first group of students to be mentors for the next group of students coming through. That has worked very effectively, so now I mainly interact with the mentors and they work with the groups. This year, I invited one of the girls who had been a mentor in the second year of the project to be a co-leader with me, and that's worked very successfully too. The student mentors develop leadership and facilitation skills for which they also receive a certificate.
> (Wendy Crebbin – Ballarat – Education, B B & P, pp. 144–145)

Ladyshewsky, R. K. (2001). *Reciprocal peer coaching: A strategy for training and development in professional disciplines.* HERDSA Guide. Canberra: Higher Education Research and Development Society of Australasia.

Computer-assisted teaching

Computers and the Web are better seen as a medium for other forms of teaching rather than a distinct form of teaching in their own right. Computer-assisted teaching can take many forms including most of those described in this chapter.

A common use of computers is for didactic teaching. Information is stored on them: lecture notes and PowerPoint files available for downloading and pages of content on the Web. The methods of computer-aided teaching described by the award-winning teachers were more oriented towards promoting active forms of learning.

Communication

Computers are very useful tools for communication, which can allow discussion to continue outside the classroom. Emails allow one-to-one or one-to-many communication, while forums facilitate asynchronous group discussions or debates. Computers, therefore, provide a medium for implementing Principle 6.1, which observes that meaningful learning is promoted by discussion.

> Web forum is suitable for shy students who would never ask questions in class nor come to me after class. Interestingly, some of these kids are very active in participating in the forum, questioning and responding. Kids nowadays are accustomed to the subculture of communicating through the internet. They like spending time at night on the web where they express themselves openly.
>
> (Chu Ming Chung – CUHK – Physics)

There was also a quotation at the end of the previous chapter which described a communication system to allow groups to discuss problem-based learning cases online.

📖   *1. E-learning 'starter guides' from the UK* by the Learning and Teaching Subject Network (LTSN) Generic Centre and the Association of Learning Technologies (ALT) (2002–2003)
Retrieved February 20, 2006, from http://www.heacademy.ac.uk/1775.htm

1. Using the WWW in Learning and Teaching
2. Virtual Learning Environments
3. Computer-mediated Conferencing

4. Using CAA to support student learning
5. Streaming Audio and Video for Course Design
6. Evaluating Learning Technology Resources
7. Integrating online learning into your course (forthcoming)
8. Approaches to evaluating the effect of ICT on student learning

2. Resources for moderators and facilitators of online discussion by
Mauri Collins and Zane L. Berge (1996–2003)
Retrieved February 20, 2006, from http://www.emoderators.com/
moderators.shtml

Cases, games and simulations

Cases were the starting point for the next example of computer-assisted
learning, which also featured simulated games.

> I have been teaching a course for undergraduates and another for post-
> graduates on ethics. I am developing some theories and principles in this
> field. I want to introduce students to dilemma situations or what moral
> reasoning is. Numerous cases will be used. . . . I use cases that students
> are familiar with such as the bribery case that *Apple Daily* had com-
> mitted with a policeman. Students certainly have read this in the news.
> They will find the case familiar and yet new in the sense that they are
> viewing it from an ethical perspective of how reporters handle such
> situations and make decisions. This case will help them get familiar
> with the situation which they may face in future as a reporter or an editor.
>
> Last summer, I applied for a courseware development grant for
> $HK50,000. I used it to make improvement in instructional design for
> a course. I picked out six cases from more than a hundred, which
> represent different ethical dilemmas. These cases were converted into
> computer-simulated games.
>
> (Kenneth Leung – CUHK – Journalism)

Simulation and games are common applications in Business.

> With computer-simulated programs, they enter some numbers and get
> some results so that they can compete with each other. There are some
> strategy games like that.
>
> (David Ahlstrom – CUHK – Management)

The simulation described in the following quotation makes Chemistry
sound much more interesting than it used to be.

We have introduced many interactive interfaces into our Computational Chemistry pages. The student can select a unique molecule, bring it up and look at it in three dimensions on the screen, manipulate it on the screen, rotate it, and then answer questions about it and its properties, or perhaps submit a job to a computational package to calculate the chemical properties of interest.

(Margaret Wong – Swinburne – Chemistry, B B & P, p. 271)

The following quotation describes a combination of simulation and role-play.

As a major experiment in developing historical empathy, I wrote a computer-simulation, Russrev, which places the student in the position of ruling post-revolution USSR. The program starts with all the factors operating in Russia in 1917 and it allows the student to take over and see if they could have done any better. Students find that you can't solve economic problems just by printing money. They find that if you have a communist government, you can't rely on overseas loans because other governments won't lend you money. Students find out that often the easiest solution is to kill the enemy. They learn that it's extremely easy to kill a million people if you can do it just by signing a piece of paper or pushing a button. I've actually had classes where somebody's yelled out, 'I've killed six million, how many have you got?' So this type of simulation develops a kind of empathy and understanding of how desperate the situation was at that time.

(Leonora Ritter – Charles Sturt – History, B B & P, p. 27)

A good general reference for games and simulations is:
Eitington, J. E. (2002). The *winning trainer: Winning ways to involve people in learning* (4th edn) (pp. 139–162). Boston: Butterworth-Heinemann.

Two which are more specific to computer-assisted games and simulations are:
Aldrich, C. (2004). *Simulations and the future of learning: An innovative (and perhaps revolutionary) approach to e-learning.* San Francisco: Pfeiffer.
Gradler, M. E. (2004). Games and simulations and their relationships to learning. In D. H. Jonassen (ed.), *Handbook of research on educational communications and technology* (2nd edn) (pp. 571–581). Mahwah, NJ: Lawrence Erlbaum Associates.

Group project

The final component of our course for teaching in higher education is a group project. Each group chooses a type of teaching – mostly one of the types described in this chapter. Each group then teaches the rest of the class about that type of teaching.

There is an expectation that the teaching and learning experiences are consistent with the chosen type of teaching. Essentially we expect a role-play of the type of teaching and we stress that a presentation about it is not acceptable. If a group picks debates, we expect them to arrange a debate for the class to participate in – not give a lecture about teaching through debates.

There is, though, an expectation that the class will learn about the type of teaching, rather than just experience it. Often one member of the group acts as a commentator describing the type of teaching, discussing options and explaining strategies for using it successfully.

Groups are formed and types of teaching chosen near the start of the course. The groups can then work on the teaching session as the course progresses. We act as facilitators for the groups and provide background material, such as the references given in this chapter. The final sessions in the course are then devoted to the group teaching. This normally provides an enjoyable climax to the course.

Chapter 12

Assessment

Influence of assessment on learning outcomes

In Chapter 8 we developed a curriculum planning model consistent with the principles derived from the interviews with the award-winning teachers. This model is shown again (Figure 12.1), because assessment is an important component of the curriculum model.

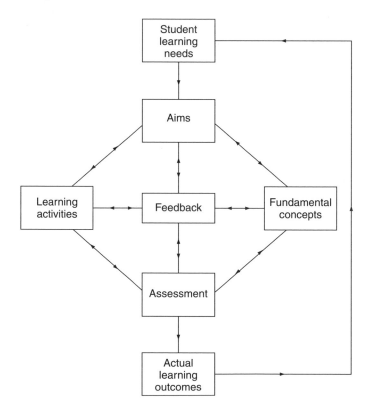

Figure 12.1

Principle 8.1 asserted that all elements of the curriculum model needed to be in concert and consistent with the desired learning outcomes, which in turn need to be compatible with eventual student learning needs. In the model diagram, assessment is shown at the base of the five elements of curriculum planning. This positioning was deliberate; so that the arrow from it appears to impinge directly upon learning outcomes. This was intended to signify the strong influence which assessment has upon actual learning outcomes. Students are assessment-driven.

> Assessment is critical because students are highly motivated, even driven, by assessment. Employers look at assessment results and grades, so students want a ticket that will get them a job. In my experience, assessment defines the curriculum for students. Since assessment drives student learning, I must carefully design my assessment packages to achieve the different learning outcomes for different subjects (and levels). I must make sure that I have an appropriate assessment system to measure my learning objectives, rather than one which purely measures recall. We can have the most wonderful aims and objectives, but unless the assessment we use encourages those objectives they won't be achieved.
>
> (Mark Freeman – UTS – Economics and Finance, B B & P, p. 43)

The implication is that assessment needs to be carefully designed to encourage the desired type of learning. Students will practise the type of learning they perceive the assessment needs. If this is not consistent with the aims, they will not be achieved.

> I have no objection to an assessment-driven learning style. It's a matter of means and ends. We should use the means, assessment, to make student learn better at the end. Assessment is part of the curriculum. We should think carefully about the function of assessment.
>
> (John Chi Kin Lee – CUHK – Curriculum and Instruction)

The corollary of assessment-driven learning is that if tasks are to be taken seriously they need to be part of the assessment. Activities with no associated marks are likely to be left undone or skipped over, unless perhaps they are seen as precursors to assessed tasks.

> You have to allocate marks to being involved in this interaction or otherwise the students won't bother. If you say to students, 'Come on, here is the facility and I think it would be a great idea if you chat with your fellow students every day because I think you'll learn by it', nobody will buy that kind of garbage. They'll say, 'Why should I? I'm a busy woman, I've got a family, I've got two children to look after at

night, I've got a husband. I've got work commitments and my weekends are taken up with other kinds of things. I'm a busy person. I don't have time to interact. Just give me the study guide and the book of readings, tell me what to do, and let me do it in my own time'. But when they get marks for reacting and commenting on other people's reflections, they know that what they're doing is useful and worthwhile, that they're not just engaging in idle chit-chat.

(Som Naidu – Southern Queensland – Education, B B & P, p. 185)

Authentic assessment

If assessment is to be consistent with desired learning outcomes and eventual student needs, it needs to be a valid or authentic task. In a professional programme a significant part of the assessment should relate closely to the eventual professional role. For a pure discipline, assessment should closely replicate the practice of the discipline.

This may sound obvious, but it is remarkable how much assessment does not follow this simple dictum. Assessment commonly tests knowledge of a discipline – and all too often recall of that knowledge – rather than the practice of the discipline.

Consistency with curriculum

If the aim of a course is for students to develop analytical ability, some, at least, of the learning activities should give practice in analysis and the assessment needs to require analysis. The gradings should reflect the level of analytical ability.

> There is no examination in this subject. I just ask students to do projects. Students have to do some analysis in their projects. Then I can examine whether the analysis is indepth and if the student is able to identify the problem. All these show how much a student has learnt. Therefore, the grade reflects how much students have learnt, and their analytical ability.
>
> (Kenneth Leung – CUHK – Journalism)

Authentic assessment can be more demanding. If students can see some point to their assignments they are more likely to put effort into it.

> We used to have a traditional exam as the final assessment in the course. We generally allocated 50% of marks to the final exam, and 50% to assignment work during the semester. Then I did away with the final exam and replaced it with a simulated job interview and written job application. I gave the students a 'job' description similar to a typical

newspaper advertisement, that required them to prepare a written application addressing certain criteria. Preparing and presenting a personal dossier/portfolio required self assessment of their own understanding and skill development in the subject area. . . . Intriguingly, when we conducted the student evaluations we found the students were well aware this was a new twist, a new game. They were also aware the assessment was designed to develop professional skills that would benefit them following graduation.

> (Chris Trevitt – ANU – Fire Science and Management,
> B B & P, pp. 293–294)

If your teaching adopts any of the methods for encouraging active learning, of the type described in Chapter 11, the assessment needs to be integrated with the learning activity. If a role-play is used, the assessment should focus on the role played by the student.

> In their essays, the students take the position of their role-play. So, if the student is playing the general, for example, his/her essay would present the position of the military on those agenda issues with which the military would be most concerned. The student may write either in the first person (assuming the role) or in the third person.
>
> (James Levy – UNSW – History, B B & P, p. 18)

The main aim of introducing problem-based learning is normally to give students practice in dealing with real-life messy problems. The assessment should be concerned with the students' resolution of the problem. If it is a test of accumulated knowledge, the point of introducing problem-based learning will be undermined.

> I have adopted a range of tools to assess problem-based learning. In this subject, assessment is not so much focused on what the student knows about the law, but about how they apply that knowledge. I am not particularly interested in them accumulating a great deal of knowledge about what the law actually is, so much as wanting them to be able to understand how the legal system functions and to be able use that knowledge for the benefit of their clients.
>
> (Peter Lee – South Australia – Social Work, B B & P, p. 112)

Consistency with professional needs

Professional courses and those which include elements of experiential learning or professional practice should have aims which relate to the development of professional competence and the display of it in the period of practice. The assessment, therefore, needs to relate to these aims.

At the end, students hand in an 'exit paper' overviewing their internship in terms of its value to them, what they learned, where it could have been improved. They also hand in whatever 'reports' they produced for their internship and describe the context in which these were produced – the briefing they received, time constraints, research involved, requirements regarding style, drafts, and background documents. In the journal and exit paper, students are expected to try to put together the theory and the practice. They read the theory and they relate the theory and conceptual material to their own experiences.

(Elaine Thompson – UNSW – Political Science, B B & P, p. 93)

The intended outcome of a management degree is a competent manager. Assessment should, therefore, relate as closely as possible to the role of a manager. This can be simulated by cases dealing with the ill-defined problems managers have to deal with in practice. Assessing knowledge of theories of management is not consistent with this aim.

My exams are mainly case-based. Seldom do I use multiple-choice or Q and A which is no more than a memory test of rote learning. The very nature of teaching business is that we do case analysis which is applied. Therefore, we assess students' understanding by judging how well they can carry out that application.

(Gordon Cheung – CUHK – Management)

Reflecting on the application of theory

Most courses teach a number of theories. A good way to test understanding of these is to set assignments which require students to apply the theories to situations they are familiar with by reflecting on their own experience.

For 'Anthropological Theories', the final paper for the people to write was: 'Pick any event which is going on in the world today; use five of these theories to explain it.' That gets students to think for themselves with any event or any personal interaction. One person described his experience working for a modelling agency, how that could be explained through these different theories. That makes the theories not abstract but directly explicit to people's lives.

(Gordon Mathews – CUHK – Anthropology)

This type of assessment is particularly effective for part-time students who are working in the field they are studying. Those in teacher education courses, for example, can reflect on how theories apply in their own schools or their own teaching.

I can give you an example of what I want in my assignments. I ask my students to examine organisations using different metaphors, different lenses of understanding it. I don't want them to simply tell me these other ways that we can do certain things. I will say, 'The first part of your paper, you've got to give me two or three pages that tell me about the context of your school. I don't mean how many students or buildings you've got, but the feeling of life in your school. Then you apply the theory to that, and you tell me what these metaphors or lenses tell you about your school.'

(Allan Walker – CUHK – Educational Administration)

Principle 12.1

Assessment must be consistent with the desired learning outcomes and eventual student needs if these are to be achieved. Assessment should, therefore, be authentic tasks for the discipline or profession.

SOLO taxonomy

The Structure of Observed Learning Outcome (SOLO) taxonomy is a classi-fication scheme which can help in both planning assessment and in providing criteria to guide grading.

I base my criteria on the SOLO taxonomy by Biggs & Collis. I explain the five levels of structural complexity that I use to determine the quality of their work and I link these levels to the grades (Fail = PreStructural, Pass2 = UniStructural, Pass1 = MultiStructural, Credit = Relational, Distinction/High Distinction = Extended Abstract). Students are given a handout that clearly identifies the criteria associated with each grade level.

For a Pass grade, I expect students to use a reasonable number of references and to portray the information accurately. I expect that their assignment will be reasonably well written and will demonstrate that they understand the content and can reproduce it. I don't expect them to give me anything new, to use the information in any way, to apply it or to make links between the bits of information.

For a Credit, students need to actually use the information rather than just write it down. They must reconstruct the information in some way to draw out principles, to make links between what various authors or writers have said, and to apply the concepts to teaching practice.

For a Distinction, students have to create something original out of the information. I'd expect their argument to follow through to some new way of looking at the material. Some students who have received Distinctions, for example, have drawn models for guiding their own practice based on the material they've written. I'm looking for a reconstruction, something original, something creative, and something personal.

(Rosalind Murray-Harvey – Flinders – Education,
B B & P, pp. 176–177)

A comprehensive guide to the SOLO taxonomy can be found in:

Biggs, J. B. and Collis, K. F. (1982). *Evaluating the quality of learning: The SOLO taxonomy (structure of the observed learning outcome)*. New York: Academic Press.

Use of SOLO for grading

The SOLO taxonomy is most commonly used as a guide to marking essays. It has five qualitative categories distinguished by the structure of the piece of writing. In the following descriptions of the categories we will use our labels rather than the original ones given by Biggs and Collis (1982). In the table on the following page the category labels are given in the first column, with our version in bold and the original beneath it.

An answer in the *missing the point* category has failed to address the issue at all. These arise in examinations when students know nothing about the question. They also occur when students mis-interpret an essay topic.

Single point answers deal with just one issue of a complex problem, though the single point may be presented in several ways. This type of answer may arise because students' schooling has conditioned them to expect problems with right or wrong answers. They, therefore, expect all questions to have single answers.

The structure of a *multiple unrelated points* essay is like a bullet point list. The material may be appropriate in answering the question, but the essay has little structuring. The points are not properly linked together. There is little in the way of introduction or conclusion to tie the ideas together. Essays like this can arise when students search for material from books or the internet and add each point to the list as it is found. The result is reproduction without interpretation.

A *logically related answer* could have the same points as a multiple unrelated one, but has a coherent structure. This time each point is related to the others so that there is a logical flow to the essay. There are introductions and conclusions which tie the essay together and provide the coherence of interpretation and argument.

An *unanticipated extension* would have the same logical coherent structure as a logically related answer. Something in the answer, though, goes beyond what the teacher could reasonably have expected. The student could have found some recent research or related theory to local conditions.

As with most qualitative categorisation schemes, the categories should be treated as a guide rather than as fixed or mutually exclusive. Judgements have to be made as to which category an essay is closest to. Intermediate cases are common. Particularly common are essays between multiple unrelated and logically related. These essays will have some degree of linking between points and an attempt at an introduction or conclusion, but not the good structure of a fully logically related answer. Answers between these points are so common that an intermediate category has been added to the following table. Intermediate positions between other categories also occur.

The SOLO category can then be used as a guide to marking assignments and awarding grades. Rosalind Murray-Harvey explained the way she allocated grades according to SOLO categories in the quotation above. Allocating grades based on SOLO means that there are criteria for grading. The final column of Table 12.1 describes the structure of an essay for each SOLO level. To translate this into a guide for grading it is just necessary to allocate a range of grades to each SOLO level.

This allocation surely provides a more satisfactory basis for marking essays than the one which seems to be most common. In the common approach the marker puts a tick every time a good point is made. The final mark then relates to the number of ticks. The problem with this semi-quantitative method is that it encourages multiple unrelated answers. Students get no credit for producing well-structured essays with a logical argument.

When the SOLO taxonomy is used as a framework for marking essays it should be treated flexibly. Essays with an intermediate structure deserve an intermediate grade. Subject knowledge also needs to be taken into account as well as structure. Even if an essay has a perfect structure, it does not deserve the grade associated with a logically related answer if it contains material which is incorrect, out-of-date or irrelevant.

Although the SOLO taxonomy is most commonly associated with essays it can also be used for marking other types of assignment. Column four in Table 12.1 shows how the categories might be applied to simple problems, complex problems, practical reports and to the outcomes of projects.

Table 12.1 The SOLO taxonomy as a guide to setting and marking assessment

SOLO category	Representation	Type of outcome	Solution to problem	Structure of essay
Unanticipated extension Extended abstract		Create Synthesise Hypothesise Validate Predict Debate Theorise	Solution to problem which goes beyond anticipated answer. Project or practical report dealing with real world ill-defined topic.	Well structured essay with clear introduction and conclusion. Issues clearly identified; clear framework for organising discussion; appropriate material selected. Evidence of wide reading from many sources. Clear evidence of sophisticated analysis or innovative thinking.
Logically related answer Relational		Apply Outline Distinguish Analyse Classify Contrast Summarise Categorise	Elegant solution to complex problem requiring identification of variables to be evaluated or hypotheses to be tested. Well structured project or practical report on open task.	Essay well structured with a clear introduction and conclusion. Framework exists which is well developed. Appropriate material. Content has logical flow, with ideas clearly expressed. Clearly identifiable structure to the argument with discussion of differing views.
Intermediate			Solution to multiple part problem with most parts correctly solved but some errors. Reasonably well structured project or practical report on open task.	Essay fairly well structured. Some issues identified. Attempt at a limited framework. Most of the material selected is appropriate. Introduction and conclusion exists. Logical presentation attempted and successful in a limited way. Some structure to the argument but only limited number of differing views and no new ideas.

Multiple unrelated points Multi-structural	☰	Explain Define List Solve Describe Interpret	Correct solution to multiple part problem requiring substitution of data from one part to the next. Poorly structured project report or practical report on open task.	Essay poorly structured. A range of material has been selected and most of the material selected is appropriate. Weak introduction and conclusion. Little attempt to provide a clear logical structure. Focus on a large number of facts with little attempt at conceptual explanations. Very little linking of material between sections in the essay or report.
Single point Unistructural	—	State Recognise Recall Quote Note Name	Correct answer to simple algorithmic problem requiring substitution of data into formula. Correct solution of one part of more complex problem.	Poor essay structure. One issue identified and this becomes the sole focus; no framework for organising discussion. Dogmatic presentation of a single solution to the set task. This idea may be restated in different ways. Little support from the literature.
Misses the point Pre-structural			Completely incorrect solution.	Inappropriate or few issues identified. No framework for discussion and little relevant material selected. Poor structure to the essay. Irrelevant detail and some misinterpretation of the question. Little logical relationship to the topic and poor use of examples.

SOLO as a guide to setting assessment

The SOLO taxonomy can also be used as a guide to setting assignments. Each SOLO level is consistent with demanding particular types of learning outcomes. Examples of these learning outcomes are shown in column three of Table 12.1. For example, the unanticipated extension category can only be achieved if assessment makes high level intellectual demands. Not all students will achieve these learning outcomes, but setting assignments at these demanding levels means that students can aim towards them.

On the other hand assessment which makes demands at the level of the 'single point' category will restrict even the most ambitious students to learning outcomes at that level. Examples of assessment of this type are numerical problems requiring substitutions into formulae. On the qualitative side are short answer questions requiring students to recall information. If all assessment for a course is constrained to this SOLO category the learning outcomes will be restricted to the level of reproductive learning.

The SOLO taxonomy can then be used as a guide to the compatibility of assessment with the other elements of the curriculum. Most importantly, the SOLO level required by the assessment needs to be consistent with the aims of the curriculum. Students will only operate at the SOLO level demanded by the assignment. If the course aims are at a higher level than the level of the assessment tasks, they will not be met.

Table 12.2 briefly reviews the advantages and disadvantages of various types of assessment. It is worth considering alternatives to those currently used.

> The following reference contains many examples of good assessment practice. The examples are organised according to eight types of capability. This makes it very suitable for finding assessment consistent with particular aims.
>
> Nightingale, P., Wiata, I. T., Toohey, S., Ryan, G., Hughes, C. and Magin, D. (1996). *Assessing learning in universities.* Sydney: University of New South Wales Press.

Variety of assessment

Achieving consistency between aims and assessment will often imply having a range of assessment items. Most courses have a number of aims and it can often be hard to devise a single item or type of assessment which tests all of the significant aims. In these cases it is preferable to have several items of assessment of different types.

I typically have four components in any assessment package. A case study or major research project usually accounts for some 25–35% of the overall grade. It's weighted so significantly because this is where students have to use their critical evaluation skills, apply theory to practice, and use computing and communication skills. It would usually be assessed by student peers and a team of staff. Students have rated this component highly as a learning task.

I usually have a final exam that is worth 40–50%, and I require students to pass this to pass the subject. The final exam has become a necessary quality control mechanism and it is widely used in this school. In the senior undergraduate subjects, I often allow the exam to be open-book format. The exam will typically consist of several components to ascertain each individual's ability to meet the objectives of the subject. At least one question requires critical thinking and the application of theoretical principles to a current issue or problem in industry. This sort of question would have no 'right' answer. Other components of the exam might include some short questions requiring evaluation (for example, identify and explain five problems with the institutional theory), calculations applying principles, and reflections on the major research project that was completed in teams. This last component is a good way of double-checking individual contributions to a team project.

The remaining one or two components in an assessment package could be in the form of team and/or individual quizzes, a mid-semester exam, rewards for continuous effort, completion of computer-based learning material, or a log book of reflections.
(Mark Freeman – UTS – Economics and Finance, B B & P, pp. 44–45)

The other advantage of having a variety of assessment items is that some can be related to learning activities. This is another aspect of achieving consistency between curriculum elements.

Asking students to demonstrate the application of learning theories in term papers is important. Small exercises will be assigned such as the following: 'Reflection papers in personal growth in teachers: Ask students to select two articles distributed in class and express their understanding'.

For in-class activities, students can use some topics discussed in class as a base for reflection. Students can be creative in showing their reflection. For example, I asked students to try something they never tried before. The rule of thumb is that the activity must not violate the law.

As an example of creative activity, some students played the role of picking aluminium cans. They asked those people who have finished playing football to give them the soda cans. The purpose of this activity

Table 12.2 Types of assessment

Assessment	Assessed	Advantages	Disadvantages
1. Traditional essay questions in examinations.	Memory of facts. Understanding of ideas. Ability to organise material. Ability to develop an argument. Original thinking.	Easy to set.	Time-consuming to mark. Marking unreliable. Poor coverage of syllabus. Favours fast and fluent writers. Limited feedback to students.
2. Pre-set essay questions.	Same as for 1.	More lifelike. Produces better level of thinking.	Same as for 1. More difficult to assess validly.
3. Open-book essay examinations.	Same as for 1. Use of reference skills.	More lifelike. Reduces stress on memorisation.	Same as for 1. Heavy emphasis on speed.
4. Essay in continuous assessment.	Same as for 1. Use of reference skills.	Lifelike task if carefully set. Reduces stress on memorisation.	Same as for 1. Possibility of collusion, plagiarism or regurgitation.
5. Short-answer written questions.	Memory for facts. Understanding of ideas, theories.	Broad coverage of syllabus. Fast marking. More reliable marking. More feedback to students.	Limited opportunity to show argument or originality.
6. Multiple-choice questions.	Memory for facts. Understanding of ideas, theories. Application of principles. Analytic thinking.	Fast marking. Reliable marking. Broad coverage of syllabus. More feedback to students.	Difficult to prepare without faults. Cannot assess skills of organising, originality or ability to solve ill-defined problems. Does nothing to develop writing skills or change conceptions of learning.

7. Oral assessment of tutorial contributions.	Oral fluency. Reasoning behind personal thought. Personal qualities.	Flexible. Useful to confirm other assessments. More valid in subjects with oral component	Very time consuming. Low reliability of marking. Difficult to standardise questions. 'Halo' effect introduces bias. Favours extroverts.
8. Presentations.	Oral fluency. Reasoning behind set topic or project. Personal qualities.	Flexible. Useful to confirm other assessments.	Very time consuming. Moderate reliability of marking.
9. Practicals.	Practical skills. Application of principles.	Only valid method for assessing such skills.	Time consuming. Low reliability of marking. Difficult to standardise questions.
10. Field-work.	Field-work skills. Application of principles.	As for 9.	As for 9, only more so.
11. Case-based learning.	Ability to analyse complex, authentic scenarios. Ability to integrate intellectual and 'working together' skills.	Develops important skills in the student. Reveals depth of thought.	Time consuming. Deciding on how to combine components of assessment can be challenging.
12. Projects. Theses.	Ability to plan original work. Ability to seek relevant information. Ability to develop an argument. Ability to draw appropriate conclusions.	As for 11.	Difficult to assess objectively. Time consuming.

is to experience the life of various people in society. Students write up the whole process. This is a training method for reflection. The reason for participating in creative activity is to let students know that I don't want students to feel homework is boring. I want students to feel some interest in homework.

(Patrick Lau – CUHK – Educational Psychology)

Individual or group activity

Return to the course plan made as an activity in Chapter 8. Add to this, at appropriate points, the assessment. Ensure that the assessment is consistent with the other planning elements – particularly the aims.

Aims	Fundamental concepts	Learning activities	Assessment

The course planning grid, including assessment, can be downloaded at http://www.routledge.com/textbooks/9780415420259.

Peer assessment

Assessment of students is most commonly performed by the teacher. It can also be by fellow students.

I randomly choose five or six of these informal reports and then I make overhead transparencies of various illustrative pages. Using these, I ask all the students in class to identify the good aspects of each report and how each one could be improved. This not only allows students to improve their performance and staff to monitor progress, but also it enables students to learn valuable skills in evaluation.

(Mark Freeman – UTS – Economics and Finance, B B & P, p. 49)

There are several advantages to peer assessment. The students can learn a great deal from the process of assessing others' work. Developing a set of criteria for a good piece of work and then applying it by marking assignments, makes students think about the qualities of a good piece of work. If the peer assessment is done in a constructive way, the appraisees benefit from the feedback. Fellow students can often provide feedback when the teacher would find it hard to cope with the number of assignments, or be in all of the locations in which the task is performed.

> Before going on prac, each student presents a case before a panel of one tutor and two peer students, and they get a lot of feedback from the panel on the way they've approached the case. I have researched the processes taking place during these peer assessments. My research indicates that students are able to mark at a comparable level to tutors. Also students are continuing to learn as they participate in the peer marking, so this assessment procedure becomes a learning process in itself instead of just being a student grading exercise. Because the marks count towards the final grade, students are given the message that their ideas are important, that they can be trusted with the responsibility of being a marker as well as a presenter.
>
> (Lynette Mackenzie – Newcastle – Occupational Therapy,
> B B & P, pp. 397–398)

📖   A comprehensive review of the various uses of peer assessment is given by:

Topping, K. (1998). Peer assessment between students in colleges and universities. *Review of educational research*, *68*(3), 249–276.

Peer assessment of contribution to group project

When group projects are used the members of a group can assess the contribution of fellow members of the group to the work and performance of the group. This exercise deals with uneven contributions. Students who contribute more are rewarded with extra marks, while freeloaders are penalised. Examination boards normally prefer differential marking of individuals to awarding each member of a project the same mark.

> Group assignments are assessed on a group basis, but with an allowance for individual contributions. When I first started doing group assignments, basically everyone in the group got the same mark and of course that didn't go over well if one student was carrying everybody

else or whatever. Now I get each person in the group to fill out a group evaluation form.

> (Stephanie Hanrahan – Queensland – Sport Psychology,
> B B & P, p. 231)

There are quite simple procedures for students to rate the contribution of other members of the group against a set of criteria. The ratings can then be used to scale the group mark for the project up or down. In this way each individual receives a mark which reflects the quality of the outcome of the project and their contribution to it.

> Students fill in a form to rate themselves and each member of their group. There are five rating criteria, ranging from creative contribution to the group to respecting the contributions of other members of the group, so the assessment of participation focuses both on process and content.
>
> (Peter Lee – South Australia – Social Work, B B & P, p. 112)

Methods for peer assessment of contributions to group projects are described in the following references. Both give sufficient detail for easy implementation. Helpful examples are also given.

Conway, R., Kember, D., Sivan, A. and Wu, M. (1993). Peer assessment of an individual's contribution to a group project. *Assessment and Evaluation in Higher Education*, *18*(1), 45–56.
Lejk, M., Wyvill, M. and Farrow, S. (1996). A survey of methods of deriving individual grades from group assessments. *Assessment and Evaluation in Higher Education*, *21*(3), 267–280.

Self assessment

Self assessment can result in similar benefits to peer assessment. Involving students in setting marking criteria is a valuable exercise as they have to think about the qualities of a good piece of work or those needed to perform a task well.

> I view self evaluation as an important part of learning. I involve students in setting goals, developing evaluation criteria, evaluating themselves and seeking feedback from critical friends. This process is both difficult and time-consuming, but well worthwhile in the long term. Students learn to focus clearly on specifics, to weigh up the importance of different aspects of the task, to plan and reflect critically.

When I give the students an assignment I spend three to four hours helping them generate the assessment criteria. They find it very difficult to get down to eight or nine criteria statements. I use snowballing in which a group of three will generate what they think the eight key criteria should be and then they get into a group of six and renegotiate and so on in larger groups. Eventually we get all the criteria up on the board. When we've decided on our six or eight criteria, we have to break each one down into the details of what they're looking for. After the students have done their assignments they assign themselves a mark on the basis of the agreed criteria. Then I give them three other (unnamed) assignments to mark and comment on. The final grade for each student's assignment is an average of (1) the person's self evaluation, (2) the average of the peer evaluations, and (3) my own evaluation.

(Dawn Francis – James Cook – Education, B B & P, p. 170)

Self and peer assessment are particularly useful in ensuring that students receive feedback in situations when it is impractical for the teacher to provide feedback to each student. Students benefit from the process of self reflection as well as the feedback.

Self assessment is a major device in helping students to develop lifelong learning skills. All students receive detailed information on assignment requirements. In their unit guides, I provide a list of 20–30 assessment criteria. On their assessment items, I require them to self-assess first, and then I give them feedback using the same scale. This enables me to point out 'perceptual gaps' where students think they have done well and I don't, and vice versa.

We videotape their workshops and they also self-assess these. Some students have felt I should look at all the videos from their workshops – but with 21 or 22 people, each doing a three hour workshop, there's just no way I could do it and stay sane or even give them any value from it. I try to persuade them that they'll be getting a wealth of data from their self assessment, their buddy's assessment, the feedback from the participants and my response to their report of the exercise – but some seem to cling to the idea that the lecturer's opinions are still worth more than their peers.

(Christine Hogan – Curtin – Management, B B & P, pp. 69–70)

Part III

Developing as a teacher

Chapter 13

Influences on good teachers

Improvement in teaching

Many, if not most, academics started their teaching careers with no formal training in teaching. Most of the existing university courses for new teachers are recent introductions.

> I remember the first time I sat in a tutorial group as a tutor with no teacher training, no orientation course, nothing. I was twenty-three or twenty-four. I walked into this room full of students, sat down and waited for the tutorial to start. I suddenly thought, 'Oh God, it's my job. I've got to start this off. How does one start a tutorial?'
>
> (Leonora Ritter – Charles Sturt – History, B B & P, p. 31)

Many of the interviewed teachers admitted that their teaching had not always been of award-winning quality, including over half of the CUHK interviewees. Indeed some had to make considerable progress to reach their current standard.

> I think what I used to do was poor teaching. I would write on the blackboard for fifty-five minutes and the students would diligently copy it down and occasionally there would be some brave soul who would ask a question – usually, 'Can I go to the toilet, sir?' – and I would think 'a job well done'. (I'd feel quite tired after writing for fifty-five minutes.) There would be no assignments, just a formal exam, and at the end of that there'd be a mark. And then I'd wonder why the vast majority of students weren't able to answer any of the questions in the exam. To my mind, that is ineffective teaching.
>
> (Michael Morgan – Monash – Physics, B B & P, p. 266)

Interestingly, the change commonly followed a similar pattern. At the start of their careers teaching tended to be didactic and concentrated on covering content. Over time the focus shifted towards aiming to ensure that students actually learnt what was important.

> When I first started teaching, I did my best to stuff students with as much content as possible. I realise that this is not the right thing to do. On the contrary, I don't need to teach so much, and I should pace my teaching so that students can truly absorb what is being taught. There is knowledge of the world that can never all be taught.
>
> (John Lui – CUHK – Computer Science and Engineering)

Another way of describing the progression is from teacher- to student-centred teaching. It seems likely that the transition was accompanied by a shift in beliefs about teaching from a teacher-centred/content-oriented belief, to a student-centred/learning-oriented one, consistent with the facilitative beliefs about teaching described in Chapter 4.

> When I first started teaching, I was very much teacher-focused rather than student-focused. I've known some teachers who are so anti-student that they really made me feel uneasy. I wanted to be different because I was interested in the students. I found that when I was interested in students they did better. As I became more confident in my ability to teach and my ability to be on top of the material, I became more aware that it was student learning that was important and that this required motivated students. I thought that if I could lock into students' own intrinsic reward system with an assessment package, or just let them have some fun, then I could motivate them to learn. So my approach to teaching changed over time.
>
> (Mark Freeman – UTS – Economics and Finance, B B & P, p. 53)

Influence of past teachers

The most frequently mentioned influence upon their teaching came from past teachers. This is perhaps not surprising as all of the interviewees must have spent thousands of hours at school and university being taught by hundreds of teachers. Some, at least, would have left a good or bad impression.

> I wasn't good at teaching at the beginning. I realised that responses from my students weren't good enough. I then tried to think of ways to improve and adopt new teaching methods. Sometimes, I will observe how good teachers teach. I have had an experience of getting ideas from observing how someone is teaching car mechanics. He taught so badly I knew what to avoid! He just talked to himself and never looked at the

students. He would continue talking without realising that his students were having difficulties catching up. Trying to learn from good teachers is a good way. Avoid ineffective teaching techniques as demonstrated in poor teaching. You need to assimilate good teaching into your own practice as you are the one who knows your class best, so appropriate modification is necessary. Be committed to make improvements.

(Andrew Chan – CUHK – Marketing)

Poor

It was possible to learn how not to teach from poor teachers. We must all have experienced poor teaching at university. Unfortunately some take these poor teachers as role models for their own teaching. Others learn what not to do and resolve to do better.

> The biggest influence on me as a teacher, I think, was the poor teaching I experienced during my own university years. I've done three degrees now and I have a doctorate. At times I've been absolutely stunned to find teachers who can actually make Social Work boring because Social Work is not a boring profession! It's stressful and dramatic and chaotic, but it's not boring! Yet so much of the social work teaching I received was absolutely and utterly boring. It wasn't the material of the profession that was boring, it was the teaching.
> (Pauline Meemeduma – James Cook – Social Work, B B & P, p. 124)

Good

Fortunately some did meet good teachers and learnt from them. Notice that in the quotation below good and poor teachers are distinguished by the same characteristics the interviewees used to describe the improvement in their own teaching. The poor teachers covered vast amounts of content, while the good teachers concentrated on students learning fundamental concepts.

> I have learnt from the few good teachers that I came across when I was a student. They explored complex knowledge in-depth and explained it to us in simple ways. They showed us how to use basic core knowledge to logically and systematically solve problems. Poor teachers would speak incessantly showing you slide after slide, giving you notes that were ten inches thick, but in the end the main themes were blurred. The good ones demonstrated the main themes within the first ten minutes of their lessons, and you would know that this is the way to approach problems. Their presentation was so clear that I can still

vividly remember the stuff being taught, and can apply what I was
taught 30 years ago to solve problems today.

(Gregory Cheng – CUHK – Medicine and Therapeutics)

Influence of colleagues

Teaching at university is often thought of as an individual activity. However,
colleagues can learn from each other.

Every morning I'll prepare coffee. You can see my coffee maker here!
My colleagues who belong to the same team for the Astronomy
course in GE will come along. We share our ideas over cups of coffee.
This morning, a colleague was saying how useful a video was for
demonstrating the telescope and how animated the students were. So
we know students' responses to various teaching aids and methods.
This is important since students differ in interest each year. Through
informal chit-chat we actually learn from each other.

(Chu Ming Chung – CUHK – Physics)

Workshops

There was some mention of courses, workshops and other educational development activities in the interview transcripts. The quotation below indicates
that one university had found a way to pass on the expertise of its award-
winning teachers.

Another strategy I have found for legitimising my practice is the Deputy
Vice-Chancellor's lunch-time sessions. These are always very well
attended. I've made sure to expose some of my ideas in his sessions.
What really helped my credibility in terms of changing other academics'
perceptions was when he introduced me one time and said, 'Now this is
one of our most innovative teachers'! Because he was giving his stamp
of approval to what I was doing, it showed that the Curtin hierarchy
confirmed, 'Yes, this is good stuff'.

(Christine Hogan – Curtin – Management, B B & P, p. 73)

There was evidence that workshops could have an impact. In Chapter 10
a quote from Soung Liew was used to describe problem-based teaching
in engineering. The impetus for this type of teaching came from a workshop.

About four years ago, I attended a three- to four-hour course organised
by the Teaching Development Unit. The course was about how to
encourage interaction with students. They called it the problem-solving
approach. I was influenced by this course. After taking the course,

I decided to include problem-solving approach discussion sessions in my course. I give them open-ended problems. They are supposed to discuss the problems among themselves with assistance from lecturers and TAs.

(Soung Liew – CUHK – Information Engineering)

Handling the teaching–research tension

Research is often cited as a detractor from good teaching. Achievements in research still tend to be more likely to result in promotion than good teaching; so dedicating time and effort to improving teaching can be seen as detracting from research performance. The award-winning teachers needed to be researchers too; so faced the tension between teaching and research like everyone else.

Enthusiasm for teaching

Even in research-intensive universities there was acceptance that the role of an academic was multifaceted. A good academic should be good at both teaching and research.

I see research and teaching as a whole package and it's not something that is separable. Just like you can't take the job, the salary and the vacations, but not the responsibility.

(John Lui – CUHK – Computer Science and Engineering)

There was genuine enthusiasm for teaching. A student-centred belief in teaching means that pleasure can be derived from students making progress.

I like teaching. Teaching is my life. I get enormous satisfaction from seeing the students grow over the four years and seeing them go out as successful teachers who are making a difference. I think that one of the things that keeps me here is when, on your very worst day when you think nothing else could possibly go wrong, some student comes along and does something absolutely wonderful. That helps me keep going.

(Dawn Francis – James Cook – Education, B B & P, p. 173)

Synergy between teaching and research

There were examples of the award-winning teachers finding a synergy between teaching and research which provided a rationale for devoting time to teaching. The first example shows how research can benefit teaching by providing real-life applications as interesting examples of the application of theory.

> Everybody is different; many of our colleagues are good teachers and they are always ranked very highly by students. They are competent and articulate and they have a language advantage. [Most of them are Cantonese speakers while Professor Fan is a Putonghua speaker.] If I am different, it is probably due to my research interest and my connection with many people in the real world. I can instantly illustrate the application of certain techniques to students with up-to-date real-life examples. For instance, the data compression technique in your digital recorder here is illustrating regression technique. An engineer can then apply and carry it over, actually program it and make the data compressed. As to that part, it is beyond our class. But the first part, the 'how' and the 'why' is within statistics. I know the technique and the application through my research and I can use it as an example to teach my students. In this way, my own research also benefits my teaching.
>
> (Fan Jianqing – CUHK – Statistics)

The second example is of teaching benefiting research. Ideas and material for publications can come from planning courses and activities in courses.

> However, the two are not mutually exclusive either. Some of my research papers are inspired by my teaching. During my teaching preparation, I will discover areas in which I want to know more. For instance, while teaching the infusion of spoken Cantonese into written text, I realize that we need some kind of benchmarking. In Hong Kong, nobody has raised this issue before. So I can publish something in this area to raise awareness.
>
> There are a couple of papers published concerning Cantonese language which are the result of my teaching. One summer, some students and I went around and interviewed a few secondary schools with approximately 200 students to investigate their phonetic problems. The result got published in an educational journal. This all started from teaching phonetics. This is to demonstrate that research and teaching are not two conflicting entities.
>
> (Chan Hung Kan – CUHK – Chinese Language)

The final form of synergy comes from teachers researching into their own teaching. Innovative teaching, which is thoroughly evaluated, can be turned into publications.

I find it's necessary to legitimise what I do with other academics and some students. One way of doing this is to publish. I research what I do in the classroom and I write it up and get it published. This is also helpful for students because the articles describe why I am using certain methods and what previous students have said about these methods. Another way of legitimising the practice is to make videos because if people see it on TV they think it's okay. I've made about ten videos.

(Christine Hogan – Curtin – Management, B B & P, p. 73)

Chapter 14

Obtaining feedback

Feedback in the curriculum development model

The curriculum development model introduced in Chapter 4 is shown again in Figure 14.1. Feedback is the central component of the model. Feedback, principally from students, can inform the development and refinement of each of the other elements in the model.

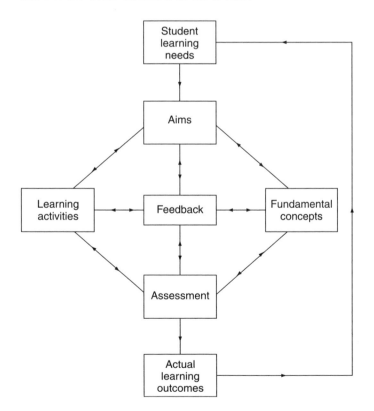

Figure 14.1

Constantly, your students are offering suggestions to improve your teaching. To resist appropriate changes is an attitudinal problem. If you are open-minded, you can make relevant improvements. Not all suggestions are reasonable. In some cases, you can modify and improve better than students suggest.

(Andrew Chan – CUHK – Management)

Good teachers should, therefore, be constantly seeking feedback with a view to improving their courses. Even the award-winning teachers were not satisfied that perfection had been reached. Further refinements can always be made. Students need change and so adaptation is necessary.

I gather feedback from students asking questions, at the end of the class, as they are unwilling to ask questions during lectures. Evaluation forms are very useful, particularly the part where students can write and express their frustrations, e.g. the project is too difficult, etc. These are much more useful than number punching. It gives you good general guidelines.

The Department pays attention to teaching. In our discussion, we talk a lot about how to improve the way we teach: forming smaller classes, getting feedback from student representatives on our courses. They do give important feedback based on which we restructure our courses to meet their needs.

(Soung Liew – CUHK – Information Engineering)

Reflection upon practice

The inclusion of feedback as a central component of the curriculum model implies a need for reflection upon practice. After classes, take time to think about what went well and could guide future practice. What did not work well and might be improved? Reflection checklists have been included in Chapters 9 and 10 to aid this reflection.

My teaching is improving continuously. I reflect upon my practice as I go along. Personally, I constantly reflect upon my teaching and seek to improve my skills almost daily. I think of ways to enhance students' learning so that they can retain the knowledge and skills for a long time and apply them appropriately. It will be great if I can make the learning process enjoyable.

(Leung Sing Fai – CUHK – Clinical Oncology)

Iterative improvement of teaching in this way can be seen as an application of the action learning cycle – planning, action, observation and reflection.

It is also akin to the developmental testing cycle used in business and engineering.

> Learning is an internalisation experience. I think action learning is important in the context of education. Reflection is also important. . . . Application of action learning is important.
>
> > (John Chi Kin Lee – CUHK – Curriculum and Instruction)

Another way of putting this is learning from mistakes. If something doesn't work, either determine how to improve it or try something else. You can also learn from your successes of course. If you learn from your successes and failures you will find that, over time, you start having more of the former.

> You learn from your mistakes as much as you learn from your successes – in fact you learn more from mistakes. I've made some monumental cock-ups in my experience as a teacher, but you've got to embrace your mistakes and enjoy them and learn from them. You've got to cherish and love your mistakes. That's what it's about, isn't it – learning from experience.
>
> > (Jim McKnight – UWS – Psychology, B B & P, p. 245)

Multiple ways of obtaining feedback

Just about all universities now require the use of teaching evaluation questionnaires on a regular basis. Many of the interviewees commented that these did not provide sufficient feedback and described other methods they used.

Many teaching evaluation questionnaires were introduced primarily for the appraisal of teachers by giving university administrations simple quantitative measures to compare teaching performance. Instruments designed with this aim in mind often provide insufficient feedback to diagnose aspects which might be improved. Relying mainly on one or two overall satisfaction items is also common, but this gives limited feedback on the multidimensional aspects of teaching.

Students also become reluctant to provide detailed feedback in response to open-ended questions unless they see action taken on their comments. Students are often asked to fill in questionnaires each semester for every course they take and every professor and instructor who teaches them. It is easy for evaluation to become a ritual to be completed as quickly as possible.

It is, therefore, not surprising that the formal evaluation conducted by universities often provides insufficient feedback for the process of curriculum development and improvement. Good teachers commonly seek out feedback themselves. The remainder of this chapter deals with ways of obtaining feedback.

Feedback in class

The first type of feedback is that obtained in class while teaching. This feedback can be used to adapt classes as they progress. It can also be used to revise future classes or make changes the next time a course is offered.

Chapter 9 contained quotations showing how good teachers monitored the expressions and behaviour of their students to see how well their classes were going. When activities are used in class, monitoring them gives insights into what has been learnt and how successful the activity was.

> There are a number of ways in which I monitor whether students are learning. In lectures, all those crowd control sorts of things tell you whether students are learning or not. You can see the glazed-eye look, you can see if they're not interacting with the material or not interacting with you, if they're not attempting the extra questions or if they're talking. Also in lectures, I look at their performance by using in-class problems.
> (Mark Freeman – UTS – Economics and Finance, B B & P, p. 49)

The interaction between students and teachers in class also provides feedback. Much of this interaction comes as a result of questions. Teachers can discover what has been learnt through their own questions. They can also learn from the questions asked by students.

> You can also get feedback in the kinds of questions that they're asking. There's no greater joy for me than to see someone put their hand up and ask a question that starts with 'So that means then that . . .' and test an inference that they've drawn. And quite frankly I don't care if they get it completely wrong. Just the evidence that they are actually going beyond the supposed absorption of information and making it part of themselves – that's what it's really about.
> (Damian Conway – Monash – Computer Science, B B & P, p. 342)

The quotation below provides a quick way to get feedback on what has been understood, or not understood, from a class. By changing the questions somewhat it is also possible to discover what extra topics students would have found valuable and what was not useful. Post-it notes are convenient for this technique.

> Occasionally I'll ask students to write down three things from the session that they didn't understand or three important things that they learned. I don't get them to put their names on the slips of paper, just to drop them in a box as they walk out. Later I'll go through

them and then at the next session I'll spend ten minutes addressing their responses.

(Marlene Le Brun – Griffith – Law, B B & P, p. 417)

Talking to students

Principle 6.2 called on teachers to develop a rapport with their students and get to know them well. If this principle is followed students will feel comfortable giving feedback on courses and teaching.

> Trust is an important element in teaching, and I try to build sufficient rapport with students to get them to tell me how we're going. I like to run focus groups in my classes and these come fairly naturally because the class is more like a discussion group than a didactic presentation. The students talk about where they're at, including what they think of the material, whether they're finding it boring or interesting or whatever. At the end of the final class we spend the last half hour talking about: How's Jim stuffed it up this time around? What could we improve? I ask a whole series of fairly detailed questions and, together with the questionnaire, that gives me a fairly good handle on my effectiveness or otherwise as a teacher.
>
> (Jim McKnight – UWS – Psychology, B B & P, pp. 245–246)

When talking to students to gain feedback use open questions so that any topic can be raised. Students will often raise issues which had not occurred to their teachers; so would not have been asked about in questionnaire items. In this way discussions with students can complement feedback from questionnaires. Discussion with students can also be used to determine what to ask in a questionnaire.

> I also speak with the students informally at the end of the subject and ask them what can be done to improve it, or what they saw as being problems. Sometimes some very trivial things are mentioned that you would never have thought of, but the students are very concerned about. For example, the students last year were concerned that the lab and the lectures were in the same week. They thought it would be better to have a gestation period of one week before they got to the labs and that suggestion was very easy to implement. These are the types of problems that they tend to bring up.
>
> (Michael Morgan – Monash – Physics, B B & P, p. 266)

Self-devised questionnaires

A simple questionnaire, similar to the one described above for obtaining feedback on classes, can be used to obtain feedback on courses. Students are more likely to give constructive feedback to open questionnaires like these than they are to formal questionnaires handed out at the end of courses. Feedback is more likely to be given if the students perceive that the teacher really wants it and is likely to respond to it.

> From time to time, I give questionnaires to students asking them to write three aspects that they like about my class and three they don't like. They can write as many as they like. These questionnaires reveal that students find the overviews in the second session most helpful because they have been given a detailed lecture in the first session. Then we can step out, strip the details and just emphasise the important.
>
> (Fan Jianqing – CUHK – Statistics)

It is also possible to devise your own questionnaires or supplement required ones with extra questions. When devising questions think what you would really like to know and what information would be useful. Devising your own questionnaires is particularly appropriate if you try forms of teaching which encourage active learning, such as those described in Chapter 11. Many teaching questionnaires assume teacher-centred or didactic forms of teaching (Kolitch and Dean, 1999), so give limited feedback when other forms of teaching are used.

> I designed my own course evaluation sheet. The main concern is whether students have enough examples. Am I going too fast in presenting course materials? Do I give enough exercises and homework, and if I give enough assistance in that respect? They really suggest I slow down and repeat and speak loudly. They requested me to put notes earlier on the internet so that they would have the notes before they come to my class. But I told them that I prefer to reorganise my lecture notes after the class so that they are more of use to students after knowing what they may find difficult and need more explanation. So my own course evaluation help me find out the small things that I was not aware of, which turn out to be important in terms of helping students understand my class.
>
> (Zhang Shuzhong – CUHK – Operations Research)

Other sources of feedback

The internet can be a good way of gathering feedback. It is more likely to be effective in courses which have regularly made use of internet discussions out of class. Some students prefer to give feedback on-line rather than talk to a teacher.

> Another idea is to set up a bulletin board on the Internet so that students can tell you whether something is succeeding or not, whether they've grasped a particular learning point or not. This is unbelievably popular!
> (Mark Freeman – UTS – Economics and Finance, B B & P, p. 49)

An advantage of internet discussions is that clarifying questions can be asked. The same applies to face-to-face discussions, but not to responses on questionnaires.

> I think this is really useful because a lot of evaluation techniques don't allow you to dialogue anonymously with the feedback-givers. But I can look at their comments and I might say, 'That's interesting, because I thought we covered that'. Then they can immediately clarify for me, and they may say, 'Well, yes you did, Chris, but things went so fast that day I didn't feel I got a grip on it'. With a lot of other end-of-semester evaluation methods, students write ideas down and they're out the door and you don't have a chance to say, 'Well, I don't really know what you mean by that', or 'Can you explain this a little further?'.
> (Christine Hogan – Curtin – Management, B B & P, p. 71)

Another medium for dialogue and feedback is the reflective journal described in Chapter 11.

> The journals are a very useful way of getting feedback from students. Because we establish a safe learning environment through the journals, students become comfortable talking to me and telling me things.
> (Keiko Yasukawa – UTS – Mathematics, B B & P, p. 305)

A questionnaire based on the principles of good teaching

Many teachers seem to find it difficult to devise good questionnaires of their own. To provide help for those who do, two versions of a course question-naire based on the principles of good teaching are shown in Boxes 14.1 and 14.2. Each principle has a scale with several items which incorporate the various facets the principle relates to. The exception is Principle 4.1, which refers to the development of generic capabilities. These are best evaluated at the programme level; so it is not appropriate to include items relating to this principle in a course questionnaire.

The first version of the questionnaire (Box 14.1) has three items per scale. The second (Box 14.2) is a fuller version with five to seven items per scale. The longer version provides a fuller and more complete characterisation of each principle and will provide more feedback. As it is longer, though, students may be more reluctant to complete it. Either version will provide diagnostic feedback indicating strengths and weaknesses with respect to each of the principles of good teaching.

Reflection on your teaching

Gather feedback through methods you find most appropriate to aid reflection upon a course you teach.

The shorter and longer versions of the course questionnaire can be downloaded at
http://www.routledge.com/textbooks/9780415420259.

Box 14.1 Course questionnaire based on the principles of good teaching

Instructions
Please mark your responses to the items below by filling up the most appropriate oval.

Use BLACK/BLUE ball pens to fill up the oval completely:

Right ●   Wrong ⊖ ⊘ ⊗ ◖

Please fill up the appropriate circle alongside the question number to indicate your level of agreement with the statements below. Please choose the one most appropriate response to each question.

⑤ – strongly agree (SA)   ④ – agree (A)
③ – only to be used if a definite answer is not possible (0)
② – disagree (D)   ① – strongly disagree (SD)

UNDERSTANDING FUNDAMENTAL CONCEPTS	SA	A	0	D	SD
1. This course concentrated on fundamental concepts.	⑤	④	③	②	①
2. In each class the key points were made clear.	⑤	④	③	②	①
3. In this course I learnt the key principles.	⑤	④	③	②	①
RELEVANCE					
4. Local examples were used to show the relevance of material.	⑤	④	③	②	①
5. I could see the relevance of material because real-life examples were given.	⑤	④	③	②	①
6. Current issues were used to make the course interesting.	⑤	④	③	②	①
CHALLENGING BELIEFS					
7. After taking this course I have a better understanding of fundamental concepts.	⑤	④	③	②	①
8. I have become more flexible in my learning.	⑤	④	③	②	①
9. I am now more willing to change my views and accept new ideas.	⑤	④	③	②	①
ACTIVE LEARNING					
10. Students were given the chance to participate in class.	⑤	④	③	②	①
11. There was discussion between students in class.	⑤	④	③	②	①
12. The teaching staff promoted discussion in class.	⑤	④	③	②	①

TEACHER–STUDENT RELATIONSHIPS

13. There was a friendly relationship between teaching staff and students.   ⑤ ④ ③ ② ①

14. The communication between teaching staff and students is good.   ⑤ ④ ③ ② ①

15. Our teacher(s) knew the individuals in the class.   ⑤ ④ ③ ② ①

MOTIVATION

16. The teacher(s) were enthusiastic.   ⑤ ④ ③ ② ①

17. I found the classes enjoyable.   ⑤ ④ ③ ② ①

18. This was an interesting course.   ⑤ ④ ③ ② ①

ORGANISATION

19. This course was well organized.   ⑤ ④ ③ ② ①

20. This course was well planned.   ⑤ ④ ③ ② ①

21. Each class was well planned.   ⑤ ④ ③ ② ①

FLEXIBILITY

22. I found teaching staff helpful when I had difficulty understanding concepts.   ⑤ ④ ③ ② ①

23. The teaching staff were sensitive to student feedback.   ⑤ ④ ③ ② ①

24. The teacher(s) were helpful when asked questions.   ⑤ ④ ③ ② ①

ASSESSMENT

25. The type of assessment related closely to the expected learning outcomes.   ⑤ ④ ③ ② ①

26. The assessment tested our understanding of key concepts.   ⑤ ④ ③ ② ①

27. A variety of assessment methods were used.   ⑤ ④ ③ ② ①

A. What was the best aspect of your course?

B. Which aspect was most in need of improvement?

Thank you for completing this questionnaire

Box 14.2 Course questionnaire based on the principles of good teaching

Please fill up the appropriate circle alongside the question number to indicate your level of agreement with the statements below. Please choose the one most appropriate response to each question.

⑤ – strongly agree (SA)   ④ – agree (A)
③ – only to be used if a definite answer is not possible (0)
② – disagree (D)   ① – strongly disagree (SD)

UNDERSTANDING FUNDAMENTAL CONCEPTS	SA	A	0	D	SD
1. This course concentrated on fundamental concepts.	⑤	④	③	②	①
2. In each class the key points were made clear.	⑤	④	③	②	①
3. We were not overloaded with a lot of facts.	⑤	④	③	②	①
4. In this course I learnt the key principles.	⑤	④	③	②	①
5. The amount of content covered was not excessive.	⑤	④	③	②	①
RELEVANCE					
6. I could understand the relevance of what was taught.	⑤	④	③	②	①
7. Theory was related to practical applications.	⑤	④	③	②	①
8. Local examples were used to show the relevance of material.	⑤	④	③	②	①
9. I could see the relevance of material because real-life examples were given.	⑤	④	③	②	①
10. Current issues were used to make the course interesting.	⑤	④	③	②	①
CHALLENGING BELIEFS					
11. In this course we were exposed to different points of view.	⑤	④	③	②	①
12. After taking this course I have a better understanding of fundamental concepts.	⑤	④	③	②	①
13. I have become more flexible in my learning.	⑤	④	③	②	①
14. There were times when the teacher(s) made us think deeply about important issues.	⑤	④	③	②	①

15. I found this course challenging.   ⑤   ④   ③   ②   ①

16. I am now more willing to change my views and   ⑤   ④   ③   ②   ①
    accept new ideas.

ACTIVE LEARNING
17. A variety of teaching methods were used.   ⑤   ④   ③   ②   ①

18. Students were given the chance to participate   ⑤   ④   ③   ②   ①
    in class.
19. There were activities which encouraged the   ⑤   ④   ③   ②   ①
    application of knowledge.
20. There was discussion between students in   ⑤   ④   ③   ②   ①
    class.
21. The teaching staff promoted discussion in class.   ⑤   ④   ③   ②   ①

TEACHER–STUDENT RELATIONSHIPS
22. I feel that our teaching staff understood our   ⑤   ④   ③   ②   ①
    learning needs.
23. There was a friendly relationship between   ⑤   ④   ③   ②   ①
    teaching staff and students.
24. The communication between teaching staff and   ⑤   ④   ③   ②   ①
    students was good.
25. Our teacher(s) knew the individuals in the class. ⑤   ④   ③   ②   ①

26. Our teacher(s) paid attention to the progress of   ⑤   ④   ③   ②   ①
    individual students.

MOTIVATION
27. The high expectations of this course motivated   ⑤   ④   ③   ②   ①
    me to learn.
28. The teacher(s) were enthusiastic.   ⑤   ④   ③   ②   ①

29. I found the classes enjoyable.   ⑤   ④   ③   ②   ①

30. This was an interesting course.   ⑤   ④   ③   ②   ①

31. The teacher(s) encouraged us to try hard.   ⑤   ④   ③   ②   ①

32. This was a demanding course but I learnt a lot   ⑤   ④   ③   ②   ①
    from it.

ORGANISATION
33. This course was well organised.   ⑤   ④   ③   ②   ①

34. This course was well planned.   ⑤   ④   ③   ②   ①

continued on next page

	SA	A	0	D	SD
35. Each class was well planned.	⑤	④	③	②	①
36. The expected learning outcomes of the course were clear.	⑤	④	③	②	①
37. The objectives of the course were clear.	⑤	④	③	②	①
38. The learning activities helped us achieve the expected learning outcomes.	⑤	④	③	②	①
39. This course catered well to our future needs.	⑤	④	③	②	①

FLEXIBILITY

	SA	A	0	D	SD
40. I found teaching staff helpful when I had difficulty understanding concepts.	⑤	④	③	②	①
41. The teaching staff were sensitive to student feedback.	⑤	④	③	②	①
42. The teacher(s) interacted with students in class.	⑤	④	③	②	①
43. The teacher(s) were helpful when asked questions.	⑤	④	③	②	①
44. Teaching was adapted in the light of student feedback.	⑤	④	③	②	①

ASSESSMENT

	SA	A	0	D	SD
45. The type of assessment relates closely to the expected learning outcomes.	⑤	④	③	②	①
46. A variety of assessment methods were used.	⑤	④	③	②	①
47. The assessment tested our understanding of key concepts.	⑤	④	③	②	①
48. The assessment was a valid test of the course objectives.	⑤	④	③	②	①
49. To do well in the course you needed to have good analytical skills.	⑤	④	③	②	①

A. What were the best aspects of the course?

B. Which aspects were most in need of improvement?

Chapter 15

Conclusion

Applicability of the principles of good teaching

The study on which this book is based used two sets of interviews with award-winning teachers. One set of 44 were selected from nominations from all Australian universities. Those selected from the pool of over 2,000 nominations were seen as being particularly noteworthy in terms of the quality of their teaching and for their ability to articulate the beliefs and practices in teaching in a way which would inform their academic colleagues. They were also selected as being representative of the categories of university and of the normal range of disciplines.

The other 18 were winners of the Vice-Chancellor's exemplary teachers' award at The Chinese University of Hong Kong during the first three years of its operation, 1999–2001. Each year one teacher was selected from each of the seven faculties of the comprehensive university. The interviewees therefore constitute a large sample of award-winning teachers from the universities in a multicultural Western country and a university in the East. The sample was representative of all major disciplines.

A rigorous grounded analysis of the stories was conducted, first with the CUHK sample. The number of verification steps was unusual. The stories were checked by the interviewees. When main themes or principles were derived, semi-quantitative measures of occurrence were noted. As each chapter was written they were examined by the interviewees for consistency with their views and practices.

The Australian sample was analysed independently, producing highly consistent outcomes. The same set of verification procedures was not feasible. Measures of occurrence were not appropriate as the Australian stories concentrated on a particular feature of the award-winner's teaching, while the CUHK ones were more comprehensive. Verification by interviewees of conclusions was not feasible because of the diverse distribution of the sample. However, the extensive quoting provides ample evidence of consistency between both sets of stories and the principles derived from the analysis.

There is, therefore, evidence that the main constructs or principles of good teaching, derived from the stories, apply well to both samples as a whole. There are also strong grounds for claiming a high degree of consistency within the samples of award-winning teachers. Given the diversity of the sample, these outcomes can be interpreted as suggesting that there is a high degree of consistency between award-winning university teachers' beliefs and practices in good teaching. Context or cultural background does not appear to be a major influence. Instead there appear to be a consistent set of principles of good teaching which apply internationally to reputable universities.

International community of university teachers

Chapter 4 argued that university academics could be regarded as an international culture. Universities and university systems have been subject to pressures towards consistency and international conformity, rather than national diversity. Globalisation of higher education has become a major theme.

Recruiting students from overseas has become a major source of income for universities in the West and universities in developing countries are now striving to do the same. Chapter 13 noted that one of the strongest influences upon academics' teaching was the teaching of their former professors. As many academics receive all or part of their education in countries other than that of their university, this provides one internationalising influence on university teaching. Of the 18 award-winning teachers from CUHK, for example, three were expatriates and 12 of the other 15 took at least one of their degrees overseas.

Another globalising influence comes from the community of the academic discipline. Networks develop through meetings at conferences which are reinforced through email exchanges. It is also possible to keep track of each other's research through journal publications.

University systems tend towards uniformity by working towards common standards. The aspirations of universities are for their performance to be of a similar standard to those recognised as being of high ranking. Universities, like the Ivy League ones in the USA and Oxford and Cambridge in the UK, therefore serve as role models for others to follow. Quality assurance practices serve to reinforce the modelling effect by setting common goals and rooting out deviations from the norm.

The external examiner system must have had a marked effect on uniformity in teaching through its aim of uniformity in degree standards. External examiners tend to be senior academics from high ranking universities. They match standards with those at their own university and others they are familiar with. Matching standards inevitably also influences what is taught and how it is taught.

It is then perhaps not surprising that a high degree of consistency with respect to what constitutes good teaching was found within the two sets of 18 and 44 award-winning teachers. It is also quite credible that the sample from the West shared similar beliefs and practices to those from the East. If academics at reputable universities share an international culture, it is quite reasonable to expect that the award-winning teachers will share common notions of excellence in teaching.

Significance of principles of good teaching

Chapter 1 observed that government bodies had sought in vain for performance indicators to measure the quality of university teaching in a way which was as easy to apply as the measures of research quality relying on numbers of publications and value of grants. As simple measures proved elusive, quality assurance for teaching has normally followed the path of what is called peer review. Assessors make judgements either on the quality of teaching itself, or on the effectiveness of a university's systems for quality assurance of teaching.

These peer reviews can be highly resource-intensive and disruptive to the department or university concerned. The reviews require the production of evidence on which the panels base their judgements. A limitation of the process is that, in the absence of readily agreed criteria for what constitutes good teaching, judgements by review panels are contestable. The, usually implicit, vision of teaching quality held by the review panel may not coincide with the values of the body being appraised.

The generation of a set of principles of good teaching from interviews with a large and culturally diverse sample of award-winning teachers does, therefore, constitute a work of significance. The principles have been empirically derived, with rigorous analytical procedures, from the beliefs and practices of academics judged to be the most effective teachers in their universities. Evidence has been produced of the wide applicability of the principles.

There are other lists of what constitutes good teaching, but the origins of these are mostly more obscure than the highly explicit derivation of the principles of exemplary teaching in this book. These principles might then be of wider application than providing a framework for a text on good teaching in universities. They have been richly illuminated by material derived from the vivid stories of the award-winning teachers.

Principles of good teaching

A fitting way to finish the book seems to be to gather together and list the principles of good teaching derived, explained and illustrated in the preceding chapters. These serve as a summary of the main conclusions of the book and a set of principles for what constitutes good teaching, which could have wide and important application.

4.1 Teaching and curriculum design needs to be consistent with meeting students' future needs. This implies the development of a range of generic capabilities including:

- self-managed learning ability,
- critical thinking,
- analytical skills,
- team-work,
- leadership, and
- communication skills.

5.1 Ensure that students have a thorough understanding of fundamental concepts, if necessary at the expense of covering excessive content.

5.2 Establish the relevance of what is taught by:

- using real-life examples,
- drawing cases from current issues,
- giving local examples, and
- relating theory to practice.

5.3 Challenging beliefs is important to:

- establish appropriate ways of learning and beliefs about knowledge, and
- deal with misconceptions of fundamental concepts.

6.1 Meaningful learning is most likely to occur when students are actively engaged with a variety of learning tasks. Discussion is an important learning activity.

6.2 Establishing empathetic relationships with students is a pre-requisite to successful interaction with them. To do this you need to know them as individuals.

7.1 Good teachers accept that it is their responsibility to motivate students to achieve the high expectations they have of them. Motivation comes through:

- encouraging students,
- the enthusiasm of the teacher,
- interesting and enjoyable classes,
- relevant material, and
- a variety of active learning approaches.

8.1 Planning programmes and courses involves consideration of students' future needs. The plans ensure that aims, fundamental concepts, learning activities and assessment are consistent with achieving outcomes related to future student needs. Feedback needs to be gathered to inform each of these elements in the curriculum design process.

8.2 Thorough planning is needed for each lesson, but plans need to be adapted flexibly in the light of feedback obtained in class.

12.1 Assessment must be consistent with the desired learning outcomes and eventual student needs if these are to be achieved. Assessment should, therefore, be authentic tasks for the discipline or profession.

References

Aldrich, C. (2004). *Simulations and the future of learning: An innovative (and perhaps revolutionary) approach to e-learning*. San Francisco: Pfeiffer.

Bain, J. D., Ballantyne, R., Mills, C. and Lester, N. C. (2002). *Reflecting on practice: Student teachers' perspectives*. Flaxton, Qld: Post Pressed.

Bain, K. (2004). *What the best college teachers do*. Cambridge, MA: Harvard University Press.

Ballantyne, R., Bain, J. and Packer, J. (1997). *Reflections on university teaching: Academics' stories*. Canberra: Australian Government Publishing Service.

Ballantyne, R., Bain, J. and Packer, J. (1999). Researching university teaching in Australia: Themes and issues in academics' reflections. *Studies in Higher Education, 24*(2), 237–257.

Barrie, S. C. (2004). A research-based approach to generic graduate attributes policy. *Higher Education Research and Development, 23*(3), 261–275.

Becher, T. (1989). *Academic tribes and territories: Intellectual enquiry and the cultures of disciplines*. Milton Keynes: SRHE and Open University Press.

Biggs, J. (1987). *Student approaches to learning and studying*. Melbourne: Australian Council for Educational Research.

Biggs, J. (1992). *Why and how do Hong Kong students learn? Using the Learning and Study Process Questionnaires*. Hong Kong: Hong Kong University.

Biggs, J., Kember, D. and Leung, D. Y. P. (2001). The revised two-factor Study Process Questionnaire: R-SPQ-2F. *British Journal of Educational Psychology, 71*, 133–149.

Biggs, J. B. and Collis, K. F. (1982). *Evaluating the quality of learning: The SOLO taxonomy*. New York: Academic Press.

Bligh, D. A. (2000). *What's the use of lectures?* San Francisco: Jossey-Bass.

Brady, L. (1990). *Curriculum development* (3rd edn). Sydney: Prentice Hall.

Collins, M. and Berge, Z. L. (1996–2003). *Resources for moderators and facilitators of online discussion*. Retrieved February 20, 2006, from http://www.emoderators.com/moderators.shtml

Conway, R., Kember, D., Sivan, A. and Wu, M. (1993). Peer assessment of an individual's contribution to a group project. *Assessment and Evaluation in Higher Education, 18*(1), 45–56.

Daly, W. T. (1994). Teaching and scholarship: Adapting American higher education to hard times. *Journal of Higher Education, 65*(1), 45–57.

Driver, R. and Erickson, G. (1983). Theories-in-action: Some theoretical and empirical issues in the study of students' conceptual frameworks. *Studies in Science Education*, *10*, 37–60.

Dunkin, M. J. (2002). Novice and award-winning teachers' concepts and beliefs about teaching in higher education: Effectiveness, efficacy and evaluation. In N. Hativa and P. Goodyear (eds), *Teacher thinking, beliefs and knowledge in higher education* (pp. 41–57). Dordrecht, the Netherlands: Kluwer Academic Publishers.

Dunkin, M. J. and Precians, R. P. (1992). Award-winning teachers' concepts of teaching. *Higher Education*, *24*, 483–502.

Eitington, J. E. (2002). *The winning trainer: Winning ways to involve people in learning* (4th edn). Boston: Butterworth-Heinemann.

Elbaz, F. (1991). Research on teachers' knowledge: The evolution of a discourse. *Journal of Curriculum Studies*, *23*, 1–19.

Glaser, B. G. and Straus, A. L. (1967). *The discovery of grounded theory*. Chicago: Aldine.

Gow, L. and Kember, D. (1990). Does higher education promote independent learning? *Higher Education*, *19*, 307–322.

Gow, L. and Kember, D. (1993). Conceptions of teaching and their relationship to student learning. *British Journal of Educational Psychology*, *63*, 20–33.

Gradler, M. E. (2004). Games and simulations and their relationships to learning. In D. H. Jonassen (ed.), *Handbook of research on educational communications and technology* (2nd edn) (pp. 571–581). Mahwah, NJ: Lawrence Erlbaum Associates.

Helm, H. and Novak, J. D. (1983). *Misconceptions in science and mathematics*. Ithaca, New York: Cornell University.

Hong Kong Education Commission (1999). *Learning for life*. Hong Kong Special Administrative Region: Education Commission.

Johnstone, D. B. (1994). College at work: Partnerships and the rebuilding of American competence. *Journal of Higher Education*, *65*(2), 168–182.

Kember, D. (1997). A reconceptualisation of the research into university academics' conceptions of teaching. *Learning and Instruction*, *7*(3), 255–275.

Kember, D. (2004). Interpreting student workload and the factors which shape students' perceptions of their workload. *Studies in Higher Education*, *29*(2), 165–184.

Kember, D. et al. (2001). *Reflective teaching and learning in the health professions*. Oxford: Blackwell Science.

Kember, D. and Kelly, M. (1993). *Improving teaching through action research*. Green Guide 14. Cambelltown: NSW: Higher Education Research and Development Society of Australasia.

Kember, D. and Gow, L. (1994). Orientations to teaching and their effect on the quality of student learning. *Journal of Higher Education*, *65*(1), 58–74.

Kember, D. and McKay, J. (1996). Action research into the quality of student learning: A paradigm for faculty development. *Journal of Higher Education*, *67*(5), 528–554.

Kember, D., Ma, R., McNaught, C. and 18 exemplary teachers (2006). *Excellent university teaching*. Hong Kong: Chinese University Press.

Kemmis, S. and McTaggart, R. (eds) (1988). *The action research planner* (3rd edn). Geelong, Victoria: Deakin University Press.

King, P. M. and Kitchener, K. S. (1994). *Developing reflective judgement: Understanding and promoting intellectual growth and critical thinking in adolescents and adults.* San Francisco: Jossey-Bass.

Kolb, D. A. (1984). *Experiential learning: Experience as the source of learning and development.* Englewood Cliffs, NJ: Prentice Hall.

Kolitch, E. and Dean, A. V. (1999). Student ratings of instruction in the USA: Hidden assumptions and missing conceptions about 'good' teaching. *Studies in Higher Education*, *24*(1), 27–42.

Kolodner, J. L., Owensby, J. N. and Guzdial, M. (2004). Case-based learning aids. In D. H. Jonassen (ed.), *Handbook of research for education communications and technology* (2nd edn). (pp. 829–861). Mahwah, NJ: Lawrence Erlbaum Associates.

Ladyshewsky, R. K. (2001). *Reciprocal peer coaching: A strategy for training and development in professional disciplines.* HERDSA Guide. Canberra: Higher Education Research and Development Society of Australasia.

Learning and Teaching Subject Network (LTSN) Generic Centre and the Association of Learning Technologies (ALT) (2002–2003). E-learning 'starter guides'. Retrieved February 20, 2006, from http://www.heacademy.ac.uk/1775.htm

Leckey, J. F. and McGuigan, M. A. (1997). Right tracks – wrong rails: The development of generic skills in higher education. *Research in Higher Education*, *38*(3), 365–378.

Lejk, M., Wyvill, M. and Farrow, S. (1996). A survey of methods of deriving individual grades from group assessments. *Assessment and Evaluation in Higher Education*, *21*(3), 267–280.

Lincoln, Y. and Guber, E. (1985). *Naturalistic inquiry.* Newbury Park, CA: Sage Publication.

Longworth, N. and Davies, W. K. (1996). *Lifelong learning.* London: Kogan Page.

McDermott, L. C. (1984). Research on conceptual understanding in mechanics. *Physics Today*, *37*, July, 24–32.

McKay, J. and Kember, D. (1997). Spoonfeeding leads to regurgitation: A better diet can result in more digestible learning outcomes. *Higher Education Research and Development*, *16*(1), 55–67.

Marsh, H. W. (1987). Students' evaluations of university teaching: Research findings, methodological issues, and directions for future research. *International Journal of Educational Research*, *11*, 253–388.

Marton, F. and Säljö, R. (1976). On qualitative differences in learning, outcome and process I. *British Journal of Educational Psychology*, *46*, 4–11.

Marton, F., Hounsell, D. and Entwistle, N. (1984). *The experience of learning.* Edinburgh: Scottish Academic Press.

Nightingale, P., Wiata, I. T., Toohey, S., Ryan, G., Hughes, C. and Magin, D. (1996). *Assessing learning in universities.* Sydney: University of New South Wales Press.

NVivo qualitative data analysis program (Version 1.3) [Computer software] (2000). Melbourne: QSR International.

Osborne, R. J. and Wittrock, M. C. (1983). Learning science: A generative process. *Science Education*, *67*(4), 489–508.

Perry, W. G. (1988). Different worlds in the same classroom. In P. Ramsden (cd.), *Improving learning: New perspectives* (pp. 145–161). London: Kogan Page.

Pratt, D. D. (1992). Conceptions of teaching. *Adult Education Quarterly, 42*(4), 203–220.

Pratt, D. D., Kelly, M. and Wong, W. S. S. (1999). Chinese conceptions of 'effective teaching' in Hong Kong: Towards culturally sensitive evaluations of teaching. *International Journal of Lifelong Education, 18*(4), 241–258.

Ramsden, P., Margetson, D., Martin, E. and Clarke, S. (1995). *Recognizing and rewarding good teaching in Australian higher education.* Canberra: Australian Government Publishing Service.

Richards, T. J. and Richards, L. (1991). The NUD–IST qualitative data analysis system. *Qualitative Sociology, 14*(4), 307–324.

Schön, D. A. (1983). *The reflective practitioner: How professionals think in action.* New York: Basic Books.

Stigler, J. and Hiebert, J. (1999). *The teaching gap.* New York: Free Press.

Straus, A. and Corbin, J. (1990). *Basics of qualitative research: Grounded theory procedures and techniques.* Newbury Park, CA. Sage.

Topping, K. (1998). Peer assessment between students in colleges and universities. *Review of Educational Research, 68*(3), 249–276.

University of Adelaide. Centre for Learning and Professional Development (CLPD) 'Leap' website. Retrieved February 20, 2006, from http://www.adelaide.edu.au/clpd/materia/leap/

University of Delaware. Problem-based learning. Retrieved February 20, 2006, from http://www.udel.edu/pbl/

University of Delaware. Problem-based learning Clearinghouse. Retrieved February 20, 2006, from https://chico.nss.udel.edu/Pbl/

Watkins, D. and Hattie, J. (1985). A longitudinal study of the approaches to learning of Australian tertiary students. *Human Learning, 4,* 127–141.

West, L. H. T. and Pines, A. L. (eds) (1985). *Cognitive structure and conceptual change.* New York: Academic Press.

Index

abstract theory 36
academic tribes 17
action learning cycle 143
action research 99
active learning 56, 57, 83
activities in lectures 80
aims 18, 66
Aldrich 112
approaches to learning 25, 29
Asian students 47
assessment 66, 115
assessment of contribution to group
    projects 94
assessment-driven 115
authentic assessment 116
award-winning teachers 2, 11

Bain 5, 12, 18, 107
Ballantyne 2, 5, 12, 18, 107
Barrie 24
Becher 17
beliefs about teaching 12, 24
beliefs: about knowledge 41; challenging
    52
Biggs 26, 31, 120
Bligh 74
boring classes 55
Brady 66
building-block approach 64

capabilities 19
case-based teaching 101
cases 111, 118
challenging beliefs 39, 43, 52
Collis 120
computer conferencing 95
computer-assisted teaching 110
computers 76

conception of learning 22
consistency 67, 116, 124
constant comparative method 2, 6
content 33
Conway 130
Corbin 6
course 19
course planning 61
course questionnaire 148
coverage 34
criteria 129; for grading 121
critical 30
critical thinking 21
curriculum design 61, 64
curriculum model 67, 114, 142
curriculum planning 63, 66

Daly 24
Davies 25
Dean 147
debate 80
debriefing 55, 90
deep approach 25
demonstrations 77
didactic approach 73
discussion 45, 83; activities 88
Driver 42
Dunkin 12

Eitington 74, 105, 112
Elbaz 2
email 45
empathy 46
encouraging students 53
enthusiasm as a teacher 54
Entwistle 26
epistemological beliefs 40
Erickson 42